The world is full of walking wounded, broken people who, once upon a time, wished upon a star, but later found themselves burned out in the cold reality of unfulfilled dreams, shattered promises, and fickle love affairs. What can be done for these hollowed-out souls, who claw their way through life begging for redemption as they eke out survival? Can they ever really live again, or are they relegated to the harsh existence of a loveless exile?

Sheri Downs's book, *What's Love Got to Do with It*, is cold water to the thirsty souls of broken people. Sheri understands the depths of despair and the hopeless feelings of betrayal. From a childhood molestation, to a fifteen-year marriage to the man of her dreams that shipwrecked on the rocks of divorce, Sheri was left to find solace for herself and her two children. In this powerful book, Sheri takes us step-by-step down the path of recovery as she teaches us how to rebuild the shelter of our souls. If you have ever been divorced, betrayed, abused, or abandoned, this book is for you. I highly recommend *What's Love Got to Do With It* to everyone who is trying to find his or her way back to joy and peace.

—Kris Vallotton
Cofounder of Bethel School
of Supernatural Ministry
Author of eight books including *The Supernatural Ways of Royalty and Spirit Wars.*
Senior Associate Leader of Bethel
Church, Redding, California

This story is the trials and triumphs of a woman not unlike you, possibly. Sheri's life can be seen in many places in many people in our society today. This book will first engage you, then challenge you and finally give you hope to find the victory for a life in Christ!

—Danny Silk
Senior Associate Leader Bethel
Church: Redding, California
Author of *Culture of Honor and
Loving Your Kids on Purpose*

I just love a great over-comer story! Sheri Downs is a powerful woman! As you read her story, you will realize just how powerful she is, *and* you will also learn how you can be powerful too! Her story is not just inspirational, it's life-giving. Her journey of overcoming is not just a testimony of God's goodness but a path for others to walk on. She gives examples of her quest to find her true identity, and through her story, you will gain a hunger for your freedom as well. Read on, but read on with anticipation of change for your own life and for those lives you influence. Enjoy her story but also be fearless to change your own.

Sheri is a blessing to all who know her, and we are happy to share her with you.

—Sheri Silk
Senior Associate Leader Bethel
Church; Redding, California

I am always intrigued by people who are thriving in life—Sheri is one of those people. What you hold in your hands is a book that is coming from someone who is truly living out the message. *What's Love Got to Do with It?* chronicles what happens when God touches a person so deeply that they will never be the same again. The result of these encounters are some of my favorite things to watch happen. Sheri's story and this book is no exception.

—Eric Johnson
Senior Leader Bethel Redding
Author of *Momentum*

It is quite brave to write about abuse, to expose it and show how it affects all those around us. The testimony of Sheri's life in *What's Love Got to Do with It?* shows the power of God's love to lead into complete freedom.

—Dawna De Silva
Founder Bethel Sozo

Sheri's honesty, determination, and courage are woven throughout this heartfelt and powerful book, *What's Love Got to Do with It?* It is a compelling account of a journey of transformation with an affirming message of hope and healing. This book is a must read for anyone who has experienced disappointment in searching for love. In its pages, you will find one woman's journey to discovering the most redemptive love story known to mankind.

—April LaFrance
Founder and CEO , OnDaySix LLC

What's LOVE Got To Do With It?

fwd by bill johnson

What's LOVE Got To Do With It?

A Journey In Search of Real Love

sheri downs

TATE PUBLISHING
AND ENTERPRISES, LLC

Published by Tate Publishing & Enterprises, LLC
127 E. Trade Center Terrace | Mustang, Oklahoma 73064 USA
1.888.361.9473 | www.tatepublishing.com

Tate Publishing is committed to excellence in the publishing industry. The company reflects the philosophy established by the founders, based on Psalm 68:11,

"The Lord gave the word and great was the company of those who published it."

Book design copyright © 2012 by Tate Publishing, LLC. All rights reserved.
Cover design by Lauro Talibong
Interior design by Ronnel Luspoc

Published in the United States of America

ISBN: 978-1-62295-833-7
1. Biography & Autobiography / Personal Memoirs
2. Religion / Christian Life / Inspirational
12.11.14

I dedicate this book to my two wonderful children, Christi and Michael. I also dedicate it to my four beautiful grandchildren: Cailyn, Alanna, Meirabel, and Kendra. Finally, I wish to dedicate it to my children's children's children. Although you will never meet me in person, you will know me in spirit because I am leaving you with a Kingdom House in which I built and dwell in!

Contents

Foreword

God places a very high value on testimonies. In fact, in Deuteronomy 6, *keeping the testimony* is mentioned alongside of His instruction for *keeping the commandment*. This implies that holding the record of what God has done is similar in value to our doing whatever He commands us to do. Reading the stories of God's grace, memorizing them, and proclaiming them are both a privilege and a responsibility. And that is where this wonderful book comes into play.

What's Love Got to Do with It? by Sheri Downs is an amazing story of God's healing love. Through her vulnerability, we read of the redemptive work of God, who brought her into a place of wholeness through His grace. This book is a powerful testimony that will touch many hearts longing to know that God loves them.

Why are books like this so important? Testimonies reveal God's nature, and the courage for radical obedience and a deep personal relationship is tied directly to our understanding of who He is. Consider this: testimonies inspire people to seek God with their whole heart as in Psalm 119:2, "Blessed are those who keep His testimonies, who seek Him with the whole heart!" What is the influence of the testimony on the heart and mind? Psalm 119:24 lets us know that they give us joy and good counsel. "Your testimonies also are my delight and my counselors." Books of this nature have the ability to ignite, inspire, and direct the hearts of many towards a deep and profound relationship with God.

Sheri's story shows us how tragedy can turn to triumph and brokenness to wholeness simply because of God's love. Her story prophesies His desire for all who make themselves available to His healing touch.

Today Sheri is one of our champions. The impact of the grace upon her life is making champions out of our students. She is experiencing a taste of God's vindication for what she has suffered. She is healed and restored, and she is bringing the same wholeness into the lives of others. I pray that the awareness of this provision of God's healing love will spread like wildfire through this story!

—Bill Johnson
Pastor – Bethel Church
Author – *When Heaven Invades Earth* and *Face to Face with God*

Acknowledgments

Thank you, Mom, for being such an amazing example in my life. You are truly my hero, and I cannot think of a better example of what real love looks like in human form. You are my inspiration.

Thank you, Janese, for always being there when I needed a friend. You are more than a friend. You are my sister, and you have seen me at my worst and still choose to be my friend. Your love and support helped to get me through the toughest time in my life, and I will be forever grateful. I prayed for years to have a sister, and God saw fit to bring you to fill that role.

Thank you, Jeremy, for being such an incredible father to my three granddaughters. And thank you for taking such great care of my baby girl and loving her the way she deserves to be loved.

Thank you, Ms. Julie Mustard, for all the many hours that you poured into this book and all your encouragement when it got difficult. We need to go on a hundred-mile bike ride to celebrate the completion of this project. I hope you don't die (like last time). Maybe just a game of tennis, so we can finally settle the tie.

Thank you, Pastor Bill, for leading a generation of revivalists that will burn throughout eternity and pouring into my life. My family lineage has been radically impacted by you.

Thank you, Kris Vallotton, for believing in me enough to hire me. You saw past my age, my divorce, and my singleness and believed in the call and anointing that is on my life.

Thank you, Mark Brookes, for being an example of what a real "dad" looks like. You have put up with me missing meetings with you because you knew I was taking care of the "kids" and I am following your example in loving these "kids" from all over the world. You're a great *dad*.

Thank you, Danny and Sheri Silk, for being such an amazing example of what a couple in ministry together look like. I have learned a tremendous amount from both of you powerful people, and when I grow up, I want to be just like you Sheri, and my husband will be just like Danny.

Thank you, BSSM staff, for allowing me to be myself and accepting me as one of the family. It is a great honor to be serving this vast army with you. I would take a bullet for any of you.

And last but certainly not least, thank you, class of 2011–2012 at BSSM. Your enthusiasm and passion have caused me to climb even higher than I thought possible. You have touched my life in more ways than I can express with mere words.

Introduction

The journey you are about to embark on within the pages of this book is a pathway that was forged by my life. As a pastor for our school of ministry, I had every intention of using our three-week break for Christmas to hit the gym and get my saggy, aging body back into a lean, strong muscle machine. The Lord had other plans for me! I would lie in bed and write for hours upon hours during our Christmas break. I never once even graced the doorstep to the gym. In fact, along with the holiday feasting and lack of exercise, I actually "gained" more incentive to get into shape (not that of a pear!). But what I did accomplish was the book that is now in your hands. It was indeed a miracle from God for me to write a book in three weeks because I do not believe that I have ever even *read* a book in three weeks!

I originally thought this would be a journal for my children and my grandchildren to leave as a legacy. I wanted my family to know me and the struggles I faced in life as well as the victories I won. As I began reliving the memories, writing them down, and processing through them, the Holy Spirit began gently prompting me to think in terms of writing a book for more than just my family to read. This thought initially scared the daylights out of me! My mind was bombarded with a plethora of questions: "Do I truly have something to say? Will anyone want to read what I write?"

Being a staff member of Bethel Church in an environment where it seems that everyone is an "author," I felt completely inadequate and somewhat intimidated by the best sellers and new releases. Nevertheless, I opened up my computer, began typing out a few ideas, and then...

Three weeks, countless cups of coffee, two tired eyes, and ten worn-out fingers later, an entire manuscript for a book was sitting in Word document form on my computer. The words just began to flow together like a well-orchestrated symphony.

In the midst of the flow, the memories came flooding, and so did the tears. It is interesting to me how much my past has influenced many things in my life, though I am not defined by it. Fortunately, in Christ Jesus we are more than conquerors, and I have shed the burial garments of pain, shame, guilt, and condemnation, and clothed myself in righteousness, peace, and joy in the Holy Spirit. God in essence, rewrote my history, and my story is being penned even to this day. It was this understanding that got me through those difficult days of putting to paper the depths of my heart and soul. Knowing that sharing my story of redemption, hope, and love could set someone else free, truly kept me motivated to press on.

Once the manuscript was complete, I began leisurely perusing books that I read and enjoyed to see how they were written. I usually only read the books to learn or to be entertained, but I quickly noticed that there were "endorsements" and "acknowledgements" and words written on the back cover to generate enough interest to open the book and read it. The thought crossed my mind, *"Sheri, what in the world were you thinking? Did you really hear from the Lord to write this book? You have absolutely no idea what you are doing!"*

It was at that point that the Lord impressed on my heart to make my book professional. My dear friend Julie Mustard helped me a great deal and was one of the key people who encouraged me to write. She actually spent many hours helping me write down my thoughts and putting words to some of my most challenging, vulnerable, and toughest memories. I can remember at one point I was out of things to write or so I thought, when Julie said, "You are not finished. You have more in you, keep writing." It felt like she was coaching me as I was running a race or competing in the Boston Marathon, and just when I wanted to quit, she was yelling from the sidelines, "You can do this! You are almost there, don't give up!" I must confess, at times I was a bit annoyed and just a little frustrated, and to top it off, this was only after the first chapter! She was a great encourager, however, and she eventually pulled the book out of me for which I am grateful.

And so it is with great honor and true humbleness of heart that I open up to you my journey. I pray that as you read my story, you will come to the same conclusion I came to in answering the question, *"What's Love Got to Do with It?"*

Part 1

The Destination Is Worth the Journey

-Introduction-

The Path Is Set

Everyone has a story to tell but not everyone is comfortable in telling it. A story is a journey to a destination. The first portion of my story may be uncomfortable for some to read. As I take you down the paths of some of my most painful memories in order to get you to the destination of my victorious present, I hope you can see the bridges and interwoven paths that all lead to a bright, hopeful future. Keep in mind as you traverse the obstacles and round some really sharp corners that all the effort will be worth it. There is, indeed, a happy ending, a dream destination, and that is exactly what has encouraged me to tell my story.

It is my desire to build hope into lives that seem hopeless and encourage all who dare to live life to the fullest even if that life threatens to leave you in despair. I am a living, breathing testimony of what happens when real love, the love of Jesus, is encountered. As you read this section, hold on to hope knowing that God is famous for taking what was meant for evil and turning it into good, and He always works *all* things together for good for those who love Him and are called according to His purposes.

-Chapter 1-

Origins

What do you do with the truth of the Word of God, when it seems contrary to your own life story? I have sometimes felt like the Bible contradicts the experiences of my life. It describes the importance, beauty, and blessing of having children—declaring that each one is special and individual. Jeremiah 1:5 speaks of our unique individuality and God's careful forming:

Before I shaped you in the womb, I knew all about you. Before you saw the light of day, I had holy plans for you: A prophet to the nations—that's what I had in mind for you. (MSG)

According to the Bible, I was not created to have something wrong with me, to have any sort of defect. I was actually created in perfection and destined to be royalty. God created my "inmost being; [He] knit me together in my mother's womb" (Ps. 139:13). Children are arrows in the quiver, and a full quiver is a blessing (Ps. 127:4–5). That is what the Bible says. However, I did not feel like an intricately knit-together child or a treasured arrow in a soldier's quiver.

The conditions surrounding my conception and birth, the early years of my childhood, and the con-

What's Love Got to Do With It?

tradictions of my life seem to sit hopelessly opposite the promise of "holy plans" and a "hope and future." Troubled by this inconsistency, I would ask, "God, where are You?" I would read Jeremiah 29:11–13:

I know what I am doing. I have it all planned out. Plans to take care of you, not abandon you. Plans to give you the future you hope for. When you call on me, when you come and pray to me, I will listen. When you come looking for me, you will find me. (MSG)

And I would ask, "God, if this promise applies to me, then where are You?" For many years, this question haunted me. As I sought my purpose in life and tried to understand why I even existed, over and over I asked, "God, where are You?" Eventually, my question set in motion a journey of discovery—to find the real meaning of intimacy and love.

Along this journey, I discovered that these promises and Bible verses are not only words in a book or good theories according to nature, but they are truths that are intricately woven throughout our lives—even in the midst of situations that set themselves in opposition to the truth. I found that in the midst of the most painful situations, the heart of God as a caring Friend, compassionate Comforter, loving Father, and intimate Lover can be most experienced.

My personal journey of overcoming pain, dysfunction, betrayal, and brokenness in the deepest parts of me was not easy, but eventually, it brought me into complete freedom and wholeness. In this place of wholeness of mind, soul, body, and spirit, I am free to dream, pursue the passions of my heart, live in convergence, and walk hand-in-hand with the Lover of my soul every day.

In order to reach this place, I had come face-to-face with the deepest, darkest places of my heart—a painful process that began with the earliest events of my life, dating all the way back to my birth. Everyone has a story, and it's not the details of the story that define us, but what we do with the details of our stories that determine who we are. The question is whether we will rise above our circumstances and overcoming impossible obstacles, knowing that our Papa God will come dashing onto the scene. Really, He has been with us all along, but we are the ones who must set our hearts on things above, where Christ is seated at the right hand of God (see Col. 3).

Now I invite you to grab a cup of freshly brewed goodness, sit back, relax, and journey with me into my story.

Unplanned

I was an unplanned baby. My parents already had their perfectly sized family of four—with two boys—and they were shocked by news of a third child on the way. This news was made even more difficult when they realized that they had incompatible blood types for child-bearing. Today, this problem is tested for prior to marriage, but back then, it was usually discovered upon the birth of the third child, who would typically have a mental or physical handicap. When it came time for me to be born, I came with complications and needed an immediate, complete blood transfusion within hours of my birth. This was such an extreme, high-risk procedure that it required both of my parents' signatures before the doctors could perform it.

At the time, my dad was working three jobs to support his growing family. This was way before cell phones and Internet access, not quite prehistoric but close, and by the time they located my dad, it was nearing the final hours before it would be too late. As a result, the doctors told my parents that I would probably be mentally handicapped. They did the transfusion, and after many extra days in the hospital, despite all the projected complications, my parents took home a new baby girl. Even in the midst of the medical uncertainties, it seems that I was destined to be on this earth for a reason; God really did create me for a purpose. But for years I would search for that purpose.

The first few years of my life were riddled with more complications that caused a huge financial burden on my family. I was a sickly child; a sniffle would turn into whooping cough, and a runny nose would end up as influenza. For the first five years of my life, I was in and out of the hospital, causing my parents added stress in their efforts to find the money to pay all the bills. One of the most severe instances happened when I contracted hepatitis at the age of five. I was a few weeks into kindergarten when I ended up isolated from my family and schoolmates, needing to be quarantined due to this disease being highly contagious. As a result, I was separated from my family even farther, every kid at school had to get a vaccination due to the severity of this disease, and when I returned a few months later, I was the bull's-eye of an easy target.

At this young age, low self-esteem first crept into my life, and I began believing a lie that I was destined to be alone. I began to construct walls of isolation and secrecy—a pattern that would follow me for many years.

A Girl in a Boy's World

Being the only female child brought other challenges in a family that consisted of boys. My parents were forced to buy me all new clothes because they could not give me hand-me-downs from my brothers. They also had to provide me a room separate from the boys and give me care suitable for a girl. My clothes were not from Macy's, but the secondhand store known as Goodwill. Still, my brothers did not like the fact that I was getting all this extra attention, and it began to put a gap between them and me. They saw me as the "favored" one; in reality, I got special treatment only because I was so weak and sickly. During those years, I began to identify with sickness, and it became a very close friend. In fact, I began believing yet another lie— that sickness is good because it got me special attention, attention that my brothers did not get. A sibling rivalry developed between us, and I was drawn farther into isolation.

The two of them would gang up on me or make fun of me when they were together; when they were with me separately, they had their own forms of treatment that usually resulted in my pain. No matter who I was with in my family, with the exception of my mom,

What's Love Got to Do With It?

I always felt like there was something majorly wrong with me.

Thus, feelings of isolation crept into my soul on a core level. At first I thought, *If I only had a sister, then I would not be alone.* But as the years passed and I realized that this was never going to happen, I decided the solution was for me to become a boy. Every night for many years I went to bed crying and praying, "God, if You love me, You will make me a boy before I wake up. If You are real, You will do this for me." I just wanted to fit in with my family. I just wanted to be normal. As the insecurity escalated, I began trying to look and act like a boy. I wore my brother's clothes, hung out with all my brothers' friends, and did all the things that boys do—including playing with cars and trucks in the dirt, throwing rocks, and playing sports.

One time, my dad decided to curl my hair to make me look more like a girl. He said, "Sheri, come here and let's curl your hair."

I replied, "I can't. I am going to play baseball with my brother."

He then retorted, "Sheri, come in here so we can do your hair. You will like it. I promise."

Giving in I said, "Okay fine," rolling my eyes and walking in the direction of the curlers awaiting me.

My dad took his time to make sure that each curler was the right temperature and was perfectly placed. It was almost intolerable for me, but I figured the sooner I got through it, the sooner I could go play baseball.

When he took the curlers out, he brushed out my hair, stepped back, and admired his beautiful daughter.

"Now that's my little girl," he said, gleaming with contentment. I, however, hated it, and ran to the bathroom to wash it all out. My dad was furious. He said, "I never want to have anything to do with your hair ever again. If you want to look like a boy, I will have no part of it!" He continued, "I thought I had two sons and a daughter, but no, I actually have three sons."

My desire to fit into my family as a boy was not working out so well for me after all. I felt terribly alone. I did not yet know that Papa God was with me the whole time; He was gently leading me down a path that would take me to Him.

Searching for Something

Even at the age of five, it was apparent that I was searching for something in every aspect of my life. In my sleep, I found myself wandering—sleepwalking around the inside of our house and even venturing out into the neighborhood. My parents watched as I ventured into different parts of the house in my sleep. It was entertaining to them at first, but it became serious when I began wandering around outside the house. They started putting furniture in front of the door to keep me from going outside, but I would somehow get around the furniture, unlock the door, and go exploring the neighborhood in my sleep.

Often, what felt like a dream to me was actually real, and when I would come to consciousness outside the safety of my home, realizing my whereabouts, I would feel scared, confused, and alone. Finding my way back to my house, I would knock on the door ever so slightly so as to wake up only my mom. I was afraid that if anyone else would answer the door, I would get into trouble for being outside. Returning to my bed, I would hope to return to sleep. This cycle continued several times a week until I was seven. Through my sleepwalking, I subconsciously tried to escape what was happening to me in my real life. Another lie entered in, the lie that I had to take care of myself. The truth that I discovered years later was that Papa was always taking care of me, and never once did I get hurt during my sleepwalking years.

My childhood search for acceptance, love, and belonging continued even as the pain, rejection, and isolation grew. Unfortunately, life in my little world got a lot worse before it got better.

-Chapter 2-

Stolen Innocence

Years later, after I was all grown-up and married, with kids of my own, around Christmas time, I was watching home movies with my parents, my husband, and my kids. They were getting a kick out of watching scenes from my childhood. One of the scenes of the movie stood out to me as important, so I asked my mom how old I was during that particular time. I remembered the house, the pool, and even the basement of the place in Maryland where I spent a few years of my life. This scene was particularly important to me because it marked one of my earliest childhood memories—the time when a trusted family member, my own brother, began sexually molesting me. I was only four years old.

I don't remember exactly how the abuse started. All I recall is being in the basement of that house in Maryland and the advent of what would become an almost-daily ritual. Pain, abuse, shame, guilt, and loss of innocence entered where joy should have lived. I was made aware of my sexuality long before any child should. The Bible says, "Do not arouse or awaken love until it so desires" (Song of Sol. 2:7). This is not to keep teenagers from doing bad things or to steal some sense

What's Love Got to Do With It?

of happiness from our lives. It is to protect us, until the appointed time, from the very thing that God created for pleasure inside of marriage. Once a person is sexualized, it is all but impossible to undo it.

The chemicals that are released into a person's brain during a sexual encounter are like a drug, and even if there is great pain involved, the body will respond to it at times with pleasure. Even in small children, these chemicals are released and activated. This is one reason why guilt and shame take such a strong foothold in children who are sexually abused. Worse than the fact that something bad was happening to me was that fact that, at times, I felt as though I actually liked it. For this reason and many others, guilt and shame played an often overwhelming role in my life.

Counterfeit Intimacy

The abuse began when I was four, and around the age of five, my abuser also introduced me to pornography. For the first time, I felt like I could identify with something, like I had something to relate to. As it was happening to me in real life, I did not know what was going on, but when I started looking at pornography, I suddenly felt like I could understand it. I even began to feel like I was accepted and loved as a result of my sexuality. After all, my childhood brain rationalized, my brother, who was supposed to protect and love me, had introduced me to this stuff, so it must be what love looks like. Surely, he wouldn't introduce something that would hurt me.

Looking at these pictures became an outlet for me from the age of five until just before I got married. The process so enveloped me that I no longer needed someone to perpetrate against me. I had found my own ways—through pornography, fantasy, and masturbation—to comfort myself. I finally felt in control of my life, or so I thought. This was another lie that it would take me years to break agreement with.

Because I was so young, I naively thought my life was following the normal course of "how things are." I thought that was just how boys and girls relate to one another. As a result, my grid for relationships, how to get attention, and how to fit in was formed around the belief that sex equals love. For all I could tell, this was the only way I could get the attention I longed for—even though it was causing me great harm. I did not realize at the time that it was harmful to me to the extent that I realized later on in life. Once I became an adult and lies were exposed, I realized just how much damage had been done during those years.

One night, when I was eight or nine years old, my brothers and I were lying on the floor watching television, and my parents were on the couch. The movie we were watching was kind of risqué for the time period in that it showed two people in bed in a sexual situation. As we were watching, my brother leaned over to me and whispered, "Don't wear panties to bed tonight."

My parents, uncomfortable with the scene, said, "This is too much for us, so we are going to bed. You kids should think about going to bed also." At that, they left the room with the movie still playing—leaving us all alone, leaving me unprotected and alone with my abuser. That night, I cried and cried, thinking to myself, *I just want my mom to hold me.* I wanted so badly to be protected. I wanted it all to stop. Unfortunately, that night like all the other nights, the abuse continued.

For many years, I carried around guilt and shame about what was happening to me in private. I did not know where to turn. I knew it must be wrong. After all, if it wasn't wrong, my brother wouldn't need to threaten me to keep me from telling others. But threaten he did. He told me I would be taken away from my family and that he would "make me pay" physically. He even said that what was happening was really all my fault. I believed him and silently endured his abuse until he entered the navy—when I was twelve years old.

Inner Healing

At twelve, I was suddenly free of my abuser, but the residual effect of those early years extended well into my adulthood. In fact, the guilt and shame stayed with me until I was thirty-four years old—when I had my first inner healing session. At Bethel Church, where I began attending in 1990 and where I am still a member today, I experienced an inner healing ministry called Sozo. In a Sozo session, lies are exposed, truth is revealed, and the walls we construct to keep ourselves safe—walls that are often deception—come crashing down. When this happens, the truth gives us the ability to walk in freedom. In my first Sozo experience, in my memories, I was taken back to a particular night when my brother walked into the room, and I knew it was going to be one of those nights.

I was rocking back and forth on my bed to help me go to sleep, as I often did, when I began to hear his footsteps. I stopped and became perfectly still. At this moment in the memory, as I was recounting it in my mind's eye during the Sozo, I saw Jesus lying in bed with me, holding me still and crying. I saw my brother enter the room, but then he turned around and walked away. This was one of the first times when I felt "covered" and protected by Jesus (see 1 Pet. 4:8). Nights free from abuse were few and far between, but that particular night, Jesus protected me from harm. The picture of Him in that moment brought healing and comfort to me, setting me on a path toward freedom from the lies, the guilt, the fear, and the shame of my abuse.

Like a Child

My childhood did not seem to set me on a path toward the Kingdom of Heaven. In Mark 10:13–16, it says,

And they were bringing children to Him [Jesus] that He might touch them; but the disciples rebuked them. But when Jesus saw this, He was indignant and said to them, "Permit the children come to me; do not hinder them; for the kingdom of God belongs to such as these. Truly I say to you, whoever does not receive the kingdom of God like a child will not enter it at all." And He took them in His arms and began blessing them, laying His hands on them. (NASB)

My childhood was full of abuse and neglect, not innocence, and I spent a good portion of my life trying to get away from being a child. Yet the Scripture says that being "like a child" is the only way to enter heaven. I realized that I needed a new understanding of *childhood*.

To me, *childhood* meant abuse, guilt, shame, neglect, and condemnation. During my Sozo, it was very important for me to go back and reclaim my early childhood years. I needed to return the innocence of a four-year-old little girl that was stolen from me. The innocence was stolen through the actions of my abuser, but the source of all that is evil is the enemy of my soul; he was the real perpetrator. I began to see the lies and deception of my youth, and I began breaking all agreements with them. For the first time, I saw the truth that, as a four-year-old little girl, I was not guilty. Actually, I was pure in heart. Through this realization, the guilt, shame, fear, and condemnation that had become my best friends in those formative years began to loosen their grip on me. Suddenly, I no longer identified with them; my identification with truth is now much stronger than the lies I once believed—as long as I continue to allow the truth to set me free.

In spite of all the things that happened to me, the truth is, I get to be my Daddy's little girl—one who is innocent, full of life, protected, and loved. Only from this posture can I enter the Kingdom of Heaven. I no longer partner with lies, but have received the fullness of the truth, and I come to my Papa, who is always eager to receive me, take me in His arms, and bless me. I can now enter into the Kingdom of Heaven and, as a child, embrace my new friends—faith, hope, and love.

Reconciliation

About ten years ago, my dad was sent to the ER because he showed symptoms of a massive heart attack. He was in the ICU, and my family was patiently waiting outside in the lounge for news of his condition. All of a sudden, my oldest brother turned his head to look at me with tears streaming down his face. We were all emotional at the time because we did not know what was going to happen with Dad, so I figured this was an expression of his pain in the moment.

Normally, he was not the type to cry, and I cannot remember ever seeing him express emotion to that extent before. He got my attention and said, "Sheri, I am so sorry for the way I treated you when we were kids. It was wrong of me, and I wonder if you can ever forgive me."

At first, I was shocked, and then my heart broke. In that moment, I realized how much he had suffered all those years. As I saw the remorse and pain in his words and tears, the memories of the abuse he endured flooded my thoughts. He too had suffered. I remembered a time when I was sitting in the truck between my dad and this brother. Accidentally, I received a blow to my head that was intended for him. Suddenly, my heart ached for him. During those years, he had suffered in ways that I will never fully understand. I looked at him and said, "Of course I forgive you."

We embraced, and true reconciliation and forgiveness took place that day. To this day, I love my brother dearly and pray for him often.

I had forgiven my brother in my heart years before that day in the hospital waiting room. It prepared me to respond with true compassion and love. Though this sort of reconciliation does not happen for everyone, forgiveness can and must. Forgiveness unlocked my own heart and released my brother.

Even when our offenders are not sorry and have never apologized, we can still forgive them. By offering forgiveness and releasing them, we are not saying that what they did was okay, and we are not excusing their behavior. Certainly, it does not mean that we have to or should trust them. Jesus demonstrated forgiveness for us when we did not deserve it and could not pay for it; in fact, Jesus forgave us before we were even repentant. He restored the standard of right-standing before God and released us from all sin. Thus, when we choose Him, we enter into the fullness of what He paid for. When we forgive our abusers, we are not only releasing them from our judgment, but we are releasing ourselves from the power and stronghold of the abuse. We are making a place in our hearts for the Holy Spirit to come and make all things new.

-Chapter 3-

Finding My First Love

Three of the four gospels recount the story of Jesus calling the little children to Himself. Because very few stories in the Gospels are recorded more than twice, we know that this one holds special significance. Luke tells it this way:

> People were also bringing babies to Jesus for him to place his hands on them. When the disciples saw this, they rebuked them. But Jesus called the children to Him and said, "Let the little children come to me and do not hinder them for the kingdom of God belongs to such as these. I tell you the truth anyone who will not receive the Kingdom of God like a little child will never enter it." (Luke 18:15–17)

This passage is key to me understanding why childlikeness is a good thing. Jesus made a bold statement with His actions by calling the children to Him. Everyone around was shooing the children away, but Jesus was calling them to Himself and demonstrating the Father's love through His actions. I needed a safe place to go. I needed Jesus to call me to Himself and show me how valued and treasured I was.

My discovery of the truth began when, at the age of eight, I accepted Jesus into my heart in my Sunday school class. I began attending the same church my grandmother went to because my cousins were the pastors. I was looking for relief from my pain even though I did not totally understand what my pain was. When I attended Sunday school for the first time, I felt love, peace, joy, and all these other emotions that I had never really known before. I could tell these people and this place were different, and it made me curious. After a few Sundays, my cousin, Dollie, led me to the Lord.

A Place to Belong

From that point on, every time the doors of the church were open, I was there. No other place brought me the kind of love and protection that I found in the people and programs of the church. I loved Sunday school and all the activities that they had for children. At one point, my cousin encouraged me to join the children's choir, and there I developed a love for singing and music and discovered that I had actually been given a gift of music.

I eagerly looked forward to children's choir, which performed at different events throughout the year. On one particular occasion, when I was about nine years old, I was picked to sing the solo for a Sunday morning special during the offering. There was a popular chorus back then called "There is a River," and I had written a verse that went along with the chorus. When it came time for my solo, I was so scared that I thought I was going to pass out. I had never sung in front of anyone by myself before, and I was terrified that I would mess up or, even worse, that people would not like me.

As I sang my solo, I noticed people throughout the congregation crying. I did not know why they were crying, but in my nine-year-old brain, I thought they were crying because I was singing horribly. When I finished my solo, I put down the microphone and sat down on the front row, not realizing that the rest of the choir was still up on the stage singing. I was so incredibly nervous that I forgot to finish the song after my part was over. The choir finished, and all my friends came and sat down with me, laughing because I didn't finish the piece.

After the service, my cousin, who was also the choir director, Dollie, came and told me that I had done a good job.

Confused, I asked her, "Why were people crying?"

She said, "That is called the anointing. When you sing, the anointing comes, and people are able to experience the presence of God. You have a gift. Sometimes when the anointing or presence of the Lord shows up, people cry."

"Then that's a good thing?" I said, still unsure.

She smiled, hugged me, and said, "That's a good thing."

I quickly realized that I did indeed have a gift—one that got me the attention I craved in what seemed like a healthy way. I also found affirmation in my relationship with my cousin, Dollie. She is an amazing woman of God, and all I wanted to do was spend time with her. She taught my Sunday school class, led the children's choir, and took me under her wing as a spiritual daughter. I spent many hours sitting with her while she played the piano. Years later I learned that my biological mom spent a lot of time hanging out with Dollie, my spiritual mom, when they were growing up. When I was with her, I would feel so at peace as she played and sang. When it came time to leave, I would always ask her, "Just one more song?" I knew that she too had a gift, what she called the anointing. I wanted to play and sing like her. She loved me unconditionally, and I knew that nothing bad would happen to me when I was around her.

My singing always put a smile on her face. Many other people liked it too, and I became accustomed to the praises of people. Many times, when I had finished singing, people would come up to me and tell me that they had felt the presence of God or that what I sang had really touched and blessed them. I liked the attention, and I liked being able to do something that made people happy. When people were happy with me, I felt good. Thus, I learned how to perform *for* love. I now know that, as my pastor Bill Johnson often says, "If you do not live by the praise of people, you will not die by their criticism."1 I wish I had known that earlier in my life. But I had no grid for it back then, and because church was the place where I experienced love and acceptance, I poured my life into the things available at the church.

Double Life

I did not realize it, but I was living a double life. At home, I lived in fear that something would happen to me if I told anyone about the abuse. My silent pain seemed to me a form of protection from what seemed like a worse fate—being taken away from my family. However, at church, I was a completely different girl. I was the perfect student who memorized scripture, showed up to everything, got all my "gold spiritual stars," and sang so beautifully that it made people cry.

Children want to be where they are loved and accepted, but they also need the love and acceptance of their natural parents. I wanted to be loved and accepted as part of my family, even if that meant keeping a secret and being abused. But on the other hand, I found love and acceptance in a spiritual family at church. The fact that I could have both lives and still function and thrive in each situation comes from the resilience that God put in each of us when He created us.

In Romans 11:27–29, Paul makes an incredible statement about this very thing. He says,

> And this is my commitment to my people: removal of their sins. From your point of view as you hear and embrace the good news of the Message, it looks like the Jews are God's enemies. But looked at from the long-range perspective of God's overall purpose, they remain God's oldest friends. God's gifts and God's call are under full warranty—never cancelled, never rescinded. (MSG)

What's Love Got to Do With It?

In the midst of pain, abuse, and a secret hidden life, I still had all that God had given to me from before the foundation of the earth. I could sing from a pure heart in church, and the presence of God would show up and His anointing would rest upon the people, and later I could go home and face the pain of that environment.

I am not saying that we should strive to live this way—quite the opposite. However, it is important for us to understand that God is not going to take away anything that He has put inside of us. The gifts and callings on our lives are the very things that He formed and fashioned in us from the foundation of the world, and they are irrevocable. God gets an immense amount of pleasure in seeing us, even if only for a second, walk in the unique gifts that He freely gave us.

Turn your eyes upon Jesus
Look full in His wonderful face
And the things of earth will grow strangely dim
In the light of Glory and Grace2

No matter what circumstance, hardship, abuse, or pain you may face, He is there. Even in the midst of the trauma of my home life, I was able to find peace, love, joy, and acceptance at church because I felt His presence there. I came alive when I was in His presence. Years later, I learned how to cultivate His presence in every aspect of my life, but as a child, all I knew was that when I was with Dollie and the other people at church or when I was singing to God, I came alive. In those moments, all the other stuff seemed not to be there, even if only for a short time. Whenever we sang that popular chorus, I felt the truth of the message coursing through my veins—so much so that I would sing it over and over and over again while I "rocked" myself to sleep. I felt His love overwhelm me every time I sang it.

Since that time, I have learned and experienced on many levels that God's gifts and callings really are irrevocable; He will never withdraw them from me, no matter what my life looks like, no matter what I am doing. In the same way, His love never fails, and He is always faithful. Everything that He has for me is good.

-Chapter 4-

Performing for Love or from Love?

Singing wasn't the only way that I found love and acceptance for what I could do. As the only girl in our family, with two older brothers, I became really good at things that boys were good at—like sports. At first, I was interested in my brothers' activities because I didn't want to be alone. They included me, but with conditions. At that time in America, girls didn't play sports, and my brothers made clear that if I wanted to play, I had to be good "or else"—meaning, that they would beat me up if I quit early or caused one of their teams to lose. I dressed like my brothers, acted like a boy, and got accolades for the things that boys were praised for. This was the origin of my identity as a tomboy, and my days as a tomboy soon began to pay off.

I moved to a different school almost every year until my sophomore year of high school. Because we moved a lot, I had to make new friends almost every year. I found that being good at sports was a way for me to fit in whether I was in Maryland or California. I was always the fastest kid at every school I attended; I was even faster than the boys. One of the schools I went to was Parsons Junior High in Redding, California, where I was recruited by the track coach after she saw me run outside during physical education. When I joined the team, I was the star athlete. I won almost every race I ran in and caused our team to win entire track meets because of the number of points that I scored. During high school, I ran so well that I graduated holding nine school records; five of those stood for over twenty-five years before someone broke them.

At the track and field state semifinals, after the end of a very close race, the incredibly tall black girl from Chico who won turned to me and said, "You are the first white girl that has ever gotten this close to beating me." That was a huge compliment since she was the only person whom I was unable to beat in our three years of competing at a high school level. She actually went on to run on the USA track and field team in the Olympics.

Because of my abilities, I was granted a scholarship to run track in college, but much to the dismay of my coaches, I decided to get married instead.

The Singing Athlete

All the kids and teachers were impressed by my ability to run like the wind, but I also played basketball and softball. Adding my athletic ability to my propensity to also win talent shows for my singing, which caused every teacher and coach to love me, made me into quite the performer. Not only was I successful in athletics, but in high school, my love for singing and music also

What's Love Got to Do With It?

started to take me places. During one of the high school talent shows, I played my guitar and sang—for which I received a standing ovation. It was the first time I had sung outside of the church, and it introduced a whole new set of possibilities. Soon I became known as the singing athlete; that was just the beginning.

My junior year in high school, I tried out for a television show called *The Morris Taylor Show*. I was only sixteen years old, and not only did I pass the audition, but I became the lead female vocalist. Every Sunday afternoon, the show was broadcast from Chico all throughout the Northern California Valley. Back then, there was no Internet or cable, and people did not have the countless options for relaxation and entertainment that we do today. If you wanted to watch television on Sunday afternoon, *The Morris Taylor Show* was one of your only options. As a result, I became somewhat popular, and people started asking me for my autograph in the most random places. I sang on the show for two years, until I was eighteen, when I decided that, though I was getting the attention that I wanted and tons of fan mail, I didn't like that my friends were teasing me about people wanting my autograph. The cycle of performance that was my public life was in full swing, and it effectively covered up all of the dysfunction that gripped my private life.

At the height of my high school success, my dad found connections with a show called *The Hee-Haw Show*, which featured Buck Owens and Roy Clark, two very well-known country and Western artists. The chance to sing on that show seemed like an incredible opportunity for larger exposure to the music world, and my dad insisted that I take it. However, I told him, "Absolutely not!" I was already getting teased about the local show, and I refused to play music that was not for the Lord. My dad was furious with me, telling me that he would no longer support my musical endeavors.

At the time, I thought I was being faithful with my gift by not compromising to sing for the world. In reality, I was so religious that I couldn't see that this was an opportunity to bring my gift into the world in a way that honored God. I was being rebellious against the wishes of my dad, and I used God as an excuse. It's ironic that I could take such an indignant, passionate stance about this issue while, at the same time, the members of my church congregation did not know about my lifestyle outside of church.

Hiding in Plain Sight

The church I attended at the time was a strict Pentecostal church a few miles from the town where I lived. As is common for this denomination, we were commanded to "come out from the world and be ye separate." There were strict rules against going to movies, watching television (let alone performing on it), violence of any kind, drinking alcoholic beverages, or any other thing having to do with the world or living life. Women had even more guidelines to follow. I was not supposed to wear pants or makeup, cut my hair, or participate in sports. Religion holds such danger. For a confused young person like myself, all of religion's rules created a false sense of security. I zealously followed

What's Love Got to Do With It?

rules in a book and walked "straight and narrow," all the while missing the real security found only in actual relationship with the Author of the Book.

Even though I was having this argument with my dad about my devotion to God, ironically, I was violating my church's rules in every other area of my life. Not only was I a female athlete who wore pants to work, but I also watched television and even performed on it. I was convinced I was going to burn in hell, and I was terrified that someone from my church would come to my workplace and catch me wearing pants. Every time someone from the church walked in the door, I would hide behind the counter until they left. If they saw me like that, it would taint my heavenly image. I didn't want them to know anything about me other than that I sang under the anointing.

Looking for Love in All the Wrong Places

Despite all of my performing for love and attention, I wasn't able to escape my deep, dark, dirty secrets. My dad was heavily into porn, and I knew where all of his books were hidden. When no one was around, I would pour over them, entering deeper into a world of fantasy and masturbation. I found some temporary relief through this private activity—which I thought no one would ever know about. When I masturbated, I felt like I was finally in control of something in my crazy, mixed-up world. I also felt like I belonged—I had found a group of people who would accept me, even if they only existed on a magazine page or in the fantasy in my head. Thus, I experienced a brief reprieve from the deep loneliness that would often overtake me.

In my double life, I performed to win love and acceptance. I didn't realize it was a counterfeit way. Real love and acceptance cannot be earned. Religion taught me that I could earn these things through performance; years later, relationship with my Creator taught me I am already loved and accepted! Ephesians 2:8–9 tells us, "For it is by grace you have been saved, through faith—and this is not from yourselves, it is the gift of God—not by works, so that no one can boast." The realization that the love I was so desperately seeking was with me all along has brought me great comfort. The truth is, even on my best day, even with my best performance, I will never be good enough to earn what Jesus gives me for free.

In Deuteronomy 31:6, Moses tells the children of Israel,

> Be strong and courageous. Do not be afraid or terrified because of them [the giants who were living in the Promised Land], for the LORD your God goes with you; he will never leave you nor forsake you.

Likewise, in the New Testament, Paul wrote to the Corinthians, "Love never fails" (1 Cor. 13:8). I am now secure in the promise of true love in its purest form, regardless of my ability to perform.

What's Love Got to Do With It?

Unfortunately, I did not yet have this revelation about true love when I embarked on my quest for my "soul mate."

-Chapter 5-

All You Need Is Love

One Wednesday night, I walked into the back of a little church on Magnolia Street. I was looking for a new church to attend. As I walked in, they were singing, which immediately drew me in. However, at the end of the song, they began singing in "tongues"—something I found just a little bit alarming. Coming from a Pentecostal background, I was accustomed to speaking in tongues, but this new use of tongues seemed a bit strange to me. I thought, *Perhaps this is one of those "New Age" satanic rituals.* At that point in my life, I was not fully aware of the supernatural aspects of God. But I knew that New Age was on the rise and that God did not want me to get involved in cults. However, before I could walk out the back door, I noticed a good-looking young man on the front row. I thought, *Well, it can't hurt to stay just a little longer.*

I met David when I was eighteen, at the end of my senior year in high school. He was sixteen and in his junior year at a very strict private Christian school. We both still lived with our parents. He came from a fairly large family of seven, which was made even bigger when his parents took in a foster family of five kids.

He first caught my eye because he fit the criteria on my checklist for what I wanted my husband to look like—tall, blond, blue-eyed, and broad-shouldered. The fact that he was a Christian pretty much sealed the deal for me.

I had also asked the Lord if I could be with someone who was an athlete and who enjoyed being physically active since that was such a large part of my life. When I found out that David was the quarterback of his high school football team, the top scorer of his basketball team, and an incredible center fielder and clean-up batter for his baseball team, I was all about "going steady" with him. I did everything I could to gain his attention. However, when we met, he was already going out with another girl, and since I was a year older than he was, I knew I would have to really pour on the charm to get him to like me.

Since I was such a great performer and knew how to get attention, I quickly put in motion a plan to get the attention of this really good-looking young man. I quickly got involved with all the youth activities and began attending all of the sporting events the church had so that I could cheer David on. When he told me what school he attended, I told him that I really enjoyed going to watch games and that I would love to come watch him play. When I started showing up at his games, his parents quickly noticed my interest toward their son, but they did not approve since I was a year older than him.

I now had to win their approval, as well as David's, so I began doing whatever I could to show them how talented I was. I became involved with the music department at the church and began singing solo numbers as the offering plate was being passed. I was an instant hit!

In time, both David and his parents grew to love me. I did not know, at the time, that I was manipulating the entire situation. Every baseball game at which I was the number one fan and every song that I sang with a glance over in his direction put me one step closer to me getting what I thought I wanted. When I decided to "pursue" David, I unknowingly put our relationship out of order. Considering all I had been through, I was in no way ready for a serious relationship, and I should have allowed him to pursue me.

Starving for Affection

I was looking for a human connection to fill a need in my life and heart that only God could fill. I was insecure and scared, and I thought that romantic attention from a man was just what I needed. All of my friends were getting married, and I desperately wanted out of my parents' house. The combination of these factors put me in a frenzied race toward marriage. If I did not hurry, I was worried I would turn into an old maid before I hit my twenties. I was not getting any younger.

In my quest for true love, I completely overlooked the fact that I was, indeed, unhealthy and starving for affection and protection. I wanted someone to take me from my dark past and give me a bright future. Instead of relying on God to do this for me, I was looking for

What's Love Got to Do With It?

my Prince Charming to come in on a white horse and rescue me. My father, who was a very controlling and stern disciplinarian, did not give me a role model for what a good husband should be, leaving me insecure, desperate, and in search of a man who would fill all of the voids in my life. I was counting on my soul mate to make me a complete and whole woman instead of recognizing that the Lover of my soul is the only one who can do this.

It took a little bit of creativity, but I finally got what I thought I wanted. The good-looking young man sitting on the front row of that little church had become a trophy of successful conquest. We were going steady.

About a year into our relationship, a new girl began attending our church, and David noticed her right away. I became very upset with him even for just smiling at her. I made it very clear by my actions that he was to have no contact with her. I tried to guilt him into not paying any attention to her. I was successful in getting what I wanted, which was all of David's attention. I had failed to realize that if I had to work so hard to rope David in, I would have to work even harder to keep him in the pen. Certainly, it was not all David's fault. What I was demanding of him was humanly impossible, and he was only nineteen years old. He was still a boy learning how to fit into a man's world and developing a sense of his own identity. Meeting the needs of another human being is difficult for anyone, let alone for a nineteen-year-old adolescent.

At one point during our courting relationship, David tried to break up with me. I fell apart and cried so hard that he did not have the heart to follow through with it. We quickly got back together, and he took on my low self-esteem and insecurity issues in an effort to somehow fix me. David had a soft heart for broken people and would attract women who were in need of a savior. This haunted us throughout our relationship.

In the midst of all of our immaturity and dysfunction, we truly were best friends. David and I always had fun together because we pursued a lot of the same passions, sharing our dreams, wants, and desires. We opened up our hearts and saw deep inside one another. We had nothing hidden in those days, and we openly communicated how our words and actions affected one another. In short, we were "falling in love." I now believe, however, that we do not fall in love, but "grow" in love; that really is what intimacy is all about. In the early days of getting to know each other, we were on to something. If I could go back and capture those times while we were dating, I would, knowing now that we were discovering, quite by accident, what true intimacy consists of.

David was the first person I felt safe enough to open up to and divulge my dirty, dark secret that I had been molested throughout most of my formative childhood years. I trusted him enough to let him into my hidden world, and I somehow thought that by telling him about all my pain and suffering, he would be able to scoop me in his arms, kiss me, and make it all go away. I thought he had the ability to stop the pain. Much to my surprise, he divulged it all to his father, breaking my trust. As a result, his father told him not to marry me

What's Love Got to Do With It?

because I was not a virgin. I also received three different warnings from people who suggested we should not
marry or should wait until we were older. Regardless,
we proceeded with our plans to marry.

During our engagement, one Sunday, our Sunday
school class took turns sharing what we each wanted to
do with our lives. I wanted to be in full-time ministry
and be a wife and a mom. I had assumed that David
wanted to be in ministry also. However, when it came
time for him to share, he stated that he wanted to take
over his dad's plumbing business and be a business-
man; he never even mentioned the ministry. I was disappointed, but I figured I could change his mind once
we were married. This should have been a *warning* sign,
but I was not to be deterred from my mission of being
married before I hit the ripe old age of twenty.

A year and a half after, I met that young man
on the front row, we married in the little church on
Magnolia Street.

-Chapter 6-

Marriage and a Baby Carriage

We began our journey together as husband and wife at the very young ages of nineteen and twenty. Looking back, I wonder, *What were we thinking?* We were just kids who were beginning to learn about how to function in the real world as young single adults. We assumed we knew how to be in a committed relationship that took time and effort to maintain and cultivate—even though we didn't even know how to balance a checkbook. *What difference does it make?* we thought. We were young and in love. We thought that would be enough.

Within a few months of our marriage, the family plumbing business that David was determined to take over was showing signs of going under, and it wasn't long before David was laid off. In the beginning, it didn't bother me because I was working at a local bank, which provided the money we needed to pay the bills. Money always seemed to be an issue and at the core of many of our disagreements, but I figured that I could work until David found other employment, and in the meantime, he could take care of the household responsibilities.

It became apparent, however, that David was not as concerned about the upkeep of our small one-bedroom

What's Love Got to Do With It?

apartment as I was. The longing I had felt for a "prince" who would ride in on a white horse and save me turned into quite another reality. I would come home from an eight-hour shift at the bank to find my "prince" still lying on the couch watching television. Meanwhile, the white horse had escaped the stable and relieved itself all over the living room floor. Or perhaps a tornado had swept through. Most nights, the apartment was a disaster, and I began to feel like my fairytale dream had turned out to be a nightmare. Certainly, it was not the life I had always dreamed about.

In response, I turned into a nag—constantly asking David to clean up or to have dinner ready by the time I got home from work. My requests went unheeded, but our discussion of household duties became a normal routine. I had no grid for what brave communication looked like, and I persistently ran from confrontation. I did not know how to properly express my needs in a way that was beneficial to both of us, and neither did he. However, our sex life was flourishing, which met some of our needs. So we simply overlooked all the others.

Perpetually Insecure

When I least expected it, my past came rushing back into my life. I had thought marrying my knight in shining armor would put it forever behind me. In reality, my past was perpetuating my present by emphasizing my insecurities. I stepped back into performance mode, and all of the images from my hours of addiction to pornography returned to haunt me. I believed that, if I could perform well in the bedroom and keep my man happy, all the other problems in our young marriage would just work themselves out. I truly believed we were intimately connected simply because we had great sex.

Throughout our entire marriage, David and I believed a lie—that intimacy is all about sex. Because of my extremely dysfunctional childhood, I thought sex equaled love, and I believed that, whenever I married, my husband would be happy with me as long as I performed well in the bedroom.

Before we married, as hormonal teenagers, we were both preoccupied with sex—a desire that culminated in our marriage union. To us, this seemed the epitome of intimacy. What we did not realize was that, in our two years of dating, we had fallen in love by spending hours together talking about our hopes and dreams. We built a strong sense of intimacy during that time, letting each other know what was going on in our hearts and not hiding anything. I had told him about the pain of my childhood, and he had also opened up his inner world before me. Thus, we developed a bond that connected our hearts long before we ever connected our bodies in marriage. In the beginning, the foundation of our marriage was true intimacy, not sex, but neither one of us realized that we needed to nurture this emotional connection consistently. Once we were married, we replaced emotional connection with physical connection and figured we'd finally found true intimacy.

Now I realize that the basis of true intimacy has little to do with sex. Certainly, sex is an important part

What's Love Got to Do With It?

of intimacy, but it is only a portion—and only between a husband and wife. God designed us to have intimacy with Him and others as well, an intimacy that has absolutely nothing to do with sex. I've heard it said that *intimacy* means "into-me-you-see." I love this definition because it paints a clear picture of what is happening when two people are intimate. I wish we had known this in the early years of our marriage.

The Good, the Bad, the Ugly

David and I had our good moments, and a significant portion of our marriage was fun. We enjoyed each other's company, had great friends, were involved in a great church, and were blessed with two amazing children— Christi and Michael. We often made one another laugh and shared similar interests; the friendship that we developed during our dating years never faded.

One night we took the kids out to dinner at a local fast-food restaurant. Christi and Michael were eight and four at the time, and we were laughing and just having fun, like we normally did. One of the patrons asked us, "Are you on vacation? There is an awful lot of laughing going on." Curious as to why a stranger would ask us this we responded, "No, but why do you ask?"

She replied, "You are having so much fun."

We simply said, "We always do."

It was true. We knew how to have fun, and to this day, I have many fun memories of our years together. However, as the years passed, the pressures of married life began to take their toll. We were too busy and too tired to spend hours sharing our hearts and dreams. We only had enough time and energy to raise our young family and deal with the daily stressors. As a result, along the way, we started to believe that, in order to appear happily married, we had to hide what we were really feeling and thinking. The routines of daily life became the walls we hid behind, and as we kept busy managing our finances, raising our children, and "going through the motions," we lost our line of communication. We stopped talking about what we were feeling in the depths of our souls. Our sex life was thriving, but we had lost the ability to dream together.

Eventually, all our hiding caught up with us. When our marriage started falling apart, David and I sought counseling, went through inner healing, and utilized all of the other tools available to us. Neither of us believed in divorce. However, we had lost our intimate connection, our ability to share what was really going on toward one another in our hearts. We focused on the fruit, but failed to expose the root that was actually dying—intimacy. We had clothed ourselves with our responsibilities and no longer granted one another access to the naked vulnerability of our true feelings.

Reflecting on what went horribly wrong in what should have been my most intimate relationship, I realize that many people go through life desperately longing for true love, but never knowing how to cultivate intimacy. True intimacy takes time, effort, commitment, patience, vulnerability, and intention. In our twenty-first–century world—a microcosm of convenience, fast-food, and microwave meals—it just sounds like way too much work.

What's Love Got to Do With It?

Maybe I was naïve, but despite our difficulties and the disconnection I felt, after fifteen years of marriage, I never expected what happened next.

The Big D

As I was leaving a counseling session where I was supporting a friend who was having a tough time in her marriage, I saw David walking toward me in the parking lot.

"Sheri," he said, "It's over! I have my things packed, and I am leaving."

Shocked, I replied, "Are you kidding me? David, what's going on?"

He repeated in what seemed like slow motion, "I'm leaving. This is not working. You will never change. You will always put other things above me."

Six months prior, David and I started undergoing some counseling. The counselor had met with us both and decided it would be best to work through my issues first, then through David's issues, and then we could work together on our marriage. We worked through many issues throughout our marriage, so this process with a counselor looked to have more hope than if we worked it out by ourselves. I was in the process of working through many of my childhood wounds when this announcement was made that he was leaving.

Until that moment, I never knew words carried such potential for devastation. Twelve little words changed the course of my life forever. The weeks following David's announcement were a blur to me. I could hardly function. My best friend and her husband, as well as my Bethel Church family, stepped in to take care of me and Christi and Michael. The harsh reality that I was going to be a single parent settled in around me. I felt like I had stumbled into quicksand and was slowly sinking—powerless and lost. After fifteen and a half years' marriage, two kids, a dog, two cars, and a mortgage, the love of my life had decided he did not love me anymore. My safe little life was suddenly turned upside down.

I had always believed I was a person who knew how to love and make others feel special. But when my lover and best friend, the one who knew me better than anyone, told me, "It's over," I began to question whether I really knew what intimacy and love were. It was the beginning of my journey into the revelation that sex does not equal intimacy and that genuine connection takes a lot of hard work and openhearted sharing.

That fateful day was also the beginning of another journey—a journey into ministry. All I had ever wanted in life was to grow up, get married, have kids, and work in full-time ministry. I had done the first two, and at the age of thirty-five, I was stepping into the beginnings of the third. Though as a teenager, David had not wanted to do church work, in the year before he left me, he had begun exploring options for full-time ministry work. When I encountered David in the Bethel parking lot, I had just finished a counseling session, along with one of the staff pastors, for a dear friend of mine. Minutes after participating in something that seemed to be the start of my ministry dream's fulfillment, I watched my dream shatter into so many pieces. Suddenly, I was no longer married; I had lost my best friend. And working in full-time ministry now seemed impossible since our denomination did not ordain divorced people. Two-thirds of my dream had suddenly vanished, leaving me bewildered and confused.

What did I do wrong? I wondered. According to everything that I had been taught in church, all the seeming success in our lives, and the connection I thought we had, I could not find a reason for such a dramatic act. I knew we had our difficulties, but neither one of us believed in divorce, and I never imagined this would happen.

During parts of my marriage, I kept a journal of what God was teaching me and some of my prayers for my life and the life of my family. Nine months before all this happened, I wrote:

> January 4, 1995: *Lord, help me to be submissive to David in everything and to not fear. You tell me in 1 Peter 3:6 to not fear. If I am following Your word and obeying Your Will, even if I doubt a decision David makes, through my prayer, submission, and support, You will work it out.*

Just two months before David left, I had a powerful encounter with God, and as a result, I wrote this journal entry:

> August 31, 1995: *I had an incredible encounter with the Lord in the form of holy laughter during my intercessory prayer group. Lord, You are so faithful and awesome. Help me to please You and not worry*

about man. Without a vision, the people perish. Thank You, Lord, for the vision of praise, intercession, and worship that You have given me. Allow me to yield my vessel to You, and let Your Spirit flow through me to others. Please take away condemnation, fear, and anything else distracting me from You.

As I would find out later, the day following my August 31 journal entry was the day when David betrayed our marriage vow. Three months after he left, I wrote this in my journal:

January 24, 1996: *Thank you, Lord, for all You are doing in me. David told me that he slept with K September 1st of last year. Was he one of those distractions that I prayed for you to take away on August 31st?*

When he called me and told me, "Sheri, I cannot keep doing this to you. I slept with K," I realized the web of lies and deceit that were being woven long before the day in the parking lot. Prior to this, I truly believed that he loved me and wanted to be with me, and if that were true, then he would have no need to be with anyone else.

Each of these entries contains specific phrases that hinted at the fact that something much bigger than I realized was going on. In my effort to be a good wife and mother, I kept submission and honoring my husband at the forefront of my mind even in my prayers and my journals. What seemed, at the time, to be innocent thoughts on paper was actually my initial discern-

What's Love Got to Do With It?

ment of what was to come. I did not recognize it at the time, which is why I was so confused when David announced his departure.

Step-by-Step

As I faced such an abrupt change, my mind wrestled with many questions. *How do I put the pieces back together and begin to dream again when so much has been lost? Can I ever realize my dreams, or am I now doomed to face the rest of my life with a big red letter painted on my chest? Can God use me ever again?* Every night I would lie awake in bed, by myself, and wonder what the shambles of my life could possibly become. I decided that pursuing intimacy with God would have to be my first step. Only He could give me the answers I needed.

Obviously, God knows everything about me, but because I was so good at denial and performance, I thought I was actually hiding my secrets from God. Little did I know that God was actually drawing me out into the open to expose the lies I had built my life around so that He could clothe me with the truth of His love. I offered up to Him all that was left within me, which was not much: shattered dreams, a broken heart, and a very dim future. As I discovered my true identity as a daughter of God, I realized that I no longer had to perform for acceptance. In exchange for all of my brokenness, He gave me hope, joy, faith, and love.

This time around, I decided that the only foundation I would build my life upon was God. I put my complete trust in Him and Him alone. The psalmist made this clear when he says in Psalm 127:1, "Unless the Lord builds the house, the builders labor in vain. Unless the Lord watches over the city, the guards stand watch in vain." I knew that I was very capable of building many things, but I no longer wanted my life to be the product of my own abilities, performance, or selfish efforts. I had tried that once. Instead, I wanted to build in such a way that the "glory of this present house will be greater than the glory of the former house" and that my house would be a place where God would "grant peace" (Hag. 2:9). This rebuilding would prove to be a multistep process.

The first step I took on my journey toward finding intimacy with God and myself was going through inner healing regarding my childhood. As I mentioned earlier, this was such an important piece that enabled me to move forward and put my life back together. I discovered that I needed to learn to completely trust God. Isaiah 26:3 says, "You will keep in perfect peace those whose minds are steadfast, because they trust in you." Until my divorce, I thought I was trusting in God. But when the pain of the divorce brought up so many other places of brokenness, I realized that I was nowhere close to completely trusting God in the way this passage describes. I was living very far from perfect peace.

Many lies that I had believed were uncovered during my Sozo, and I began facing the pain I had endured as a child. For so many years, I had covered up and denied what had happened. So the first thing I had to do was take an honest look within and release myself from the guilt and shame that had become my best

What's Love Got to Do With It?

friends. Once I did that, I was able to see myself as God created me. Instead of carrying around a deep, dark, dirty little secret, I was free to be me, no longer needing to perform in order to be accepted. I was able to embrace the truth that I am an innocent, pure, beautiful, fun, joyful pleasure to be around.

Learning to Trust

The next step was learning to trust people again—which was not easy. I certainly believe in healthy boundaries, but I had taken boundaries to a whole new level by constructing walls that would keep me safe from anyone ever hurting me again. The problem was that the walls I had built to keep myself safe simply isolated me by keeping people out. Inside, I was still dying a slow death even though I had received so much love and freedom from being intimate with God and myself. The Lord showed me that in order for me to continue to walk out my freedom, I needed to begin letting people in and experiencing intimacy with other humans.

This meant taking risks and opening up to those who could possibly hurt me and cause me more pain. As I wrestled with this next step, I realized that these walls had been the strategy of the enemy to keep me isolated—making me think I could only live life on a surface level with the very people God had given to me to be my intimate friends. The solution hinged on the revelation that I needed to surround myself with people who would love me for me because what I was *actually* longing for was true intimacy with others.

We have all been created for community and cannot be fully functioning apart from it. When speaking to the Colossians, Paul admonished them by saying,

Therefore as God's chosen people, holy and dearly loved, clothe yourselves with compassion, kindness, humility, gentleness, and patience. Bear with each other and forgive one another if any of you has a grievance against someone. Forgive as the Lord forgave you. And over all these virtues, put on love, which binds them all together in perfect unity. Let the peace of Christ rule in your hearts, since as members of one body you were called to peace. And be thankful. (Col. 3:12–15)

I needed to intentionally choose intimacy in community, not just expect that it would just happen to me.

Transitions

The same year that David left, another shift began to happen in my world that further challenged the whole concept of trusting people. The pastor of my church stepped down from his position, and it was not long before my Bethel Church family began taking on a new look. Little by little, I watched as the people whom I had worshipped with for the past several years—many of whom had helped me through my divorce—began an exodus.

A radical pastor named Bill Johnson, who pastored a church in Weaverville, California, was invited to apply for the open senior pastor role at Bethel Church. In 1994, revival broke out in Toronto, Canada,—what would later be termed the Toronto Blessing—and Bill had traveled there and brought the revival back to his

What's Love Got to Do With It?

church in Weaverville. When Bethel Church heard of it, they invited him to come to Redding. I knew of Bill because his father, Earl Johnson, had been the pastor of Bethel Church years earlier, and Earl and his wife were still members of our congregation. Also, Bill's sister, Jacque, was a friend of mine. When Bill came and spoke at our choir retreat, I became completely sold out to the message of his life. He released the presence of God when he sat at the piano and led us in worship. Then he spoke, the revelation that came out of his mouth floored me. His words brought new life to my spirit and awakened me with fresh fire.

As a voting member of the church, I was certain that everyone would agree with me and vote in Bill as our new pastor. I was right; he received unanimous agreement that he was the man for the position. I was excited, as everyone seemed to be, and much anticipation filled the atmosphere. However, I was completely unprepared for what was about to take place next.

Bill often spoke about how revival can be messy, but he never backed down or apologized for what was happening in our meetings. He was also gracious and gentle, and instead of springing everything on the entire congregation at once, he began implementing a revival culture first among the leaders. I was not a leader at the time, so I was not at those initial meetings where the leaders were experiencing encounters with the Lord, but I certainly heard about them.

It was not long before our Sunday night meetings became fertile ground for revival to burst forth. Bill and the leadership team began to give freedom to the moving of the Holy Spirit, and the miracles started exploding in our midst; heaven was beginning to invade. One Sunday night, I witnessed a paralyzed man, who had been coming to the church for several months, get up out of his wheelchair and walk for the first time in years! I burst into tears of rejoicing.

A phenomenon called holy laughter also broke out in our midst, and people began to be "slain in the Spirit"—something I hadn't seen in years. I was thrilled with what was taking place, and during that season I had my own special encounters that literally changed the course of my life. In one of my most powerful encounters with Jesus, I saw Him betroth Himself to me and place a ring on my finger (a story that I tell in more detail in the next chapter).

I also received a very nice guitar during one of our Holy Spirit "swap meets" where people would give certain things to other people based on how they felt the Lord guiding them. On the night when I received the blond Takamine guitar, something changed; my love for music experienced a rebirth in me, and I began to worship in a way that I had not since my divorce. Unknowingly, in the pain of David's rejection, I had allowed that part of me to die, but in God's kindness, He had sent me a guitar to remind me that I loved to sing to Him.

Bill often said, "Follow where the Lord is moving," and that was what he had done when he traveled to receive from what God was doing in Toronto. I, however, had prayed for the Lord to begin moving in Redding because, as a single mom, I could barely

What's Love Got to Do With It?

afford a trip to the movies, let alone travel to places that were experiencing revival—like Toronto, Canada, and Brownsville, Florida. Just as I had prayed, when Bill and Beni Johnson came to Bethel, revival came too. Yet so many people were leaving the church due to the unfamiliar manifestations that were taking place. I felt a bit confused. The Lord was showing up in powerful ways—which was exactly what so many of us had been praying for. *Now that it is happening, why is everyone leaving?* I wondered.

As things were changing in the congregation, a new opportunity arose. Bethel Church decided to start a ministry school—Bethel School of Supernatural Ministry. *Is this my chance to get trained for full-time ministry?* I wondered. It seemed like such an amazing opportunity, but financially, it felt impossible. *There is no way I will be able to afford to go back to school. I have to raise my kids and make a living,* I told myself. But the desire never loosened its grip, and by the time the school was in its third year, I decided it was time for me to trust God at a whole new level and to start trusting people.

Worth the Risk

Deciding that true intimacy with others was worth the risk, I took a step of faith and immersed myself in the church culture and the Bethel School of Supernatural Ministry. I became a student and began building relationships with those who had the same passion for the presence of the Lord, a passion that still has my affections today. Even though it was challenging for me at first, I built some lifelong friendships by opening myself up to intimacy with others and allowing them to see inside of me. Much to my surprise, I discovered that they love the real me. It is extremely refreshing and rewarding to know I can be real with those the Lord has put in my life. I know they will confront me in love when necessary, ask me tough questions when it is uncomfortable, and not let me get away with hiding behind walls of isolation—all from a foundation of acceptance and love.

I have discovered the true meaning of intimacy with God, myself, and those God has placed in my life. I am no longer afraid of being vulnerable or real, and I am cultivating this daily by making it a lifestyle, one propagated by daily communing with Papa God. This takes on various forms, but tangibly consists of personal time with Him through worship, quiet time, and reading the Word, being intentional about building true relationships with those around me, creating a safe place for others to be real, and genuinely loving people the way Papa God, the Holy Spirit, and Jesus love me.

For a person who had major trust issues and a broken and warped sense of intimacy, I have had tremendous breakthrough. I am quite confident that if my paradigm can make such a drastic shift, then all who are willing to open up and be real with God, themselves, and others will also experience a whole new world of love and true intimacy, no matter what their circumstances.

What's Love Got to Do With It?

-Chapter 7-

My Buddies and Me

My buddies, my buddies,
I take 'em everywhere I go.
My buddies, my buddies,
I teach 'em everything I know.
My buddies and me like to climb up a tree.
My buddies and me we're the best friends can be.
My buddies, my buddies, my buddies and me.

After David left, I would sing this song to my kids. It was just the three of us now even though we prayed every night for daddy to come home. Over the next few years, I prayed and believed that God could restore our relationship and bring David back to me.

Then one Saturday morning, about a year after he had left, I received a phone call from him. He said, "Sheri, I finally met the woman of my dreams. We are going to get married. Can the kids come out for a couple of weeks in the summer to meet her?"

Months later, standing in the Sacramento airport with my best friend, I watched the plane take off, carrying my two babies, who had never flown before, into a world foreign even to me—Las Vegas, Nevada. I watched the plane until it disappeared into the sky, and as we drove two and a half hours back to Redding, I cried myself to sleep.

Two weeks later, when we went to pick them up, both Michael and Christi came off the plane happy to see me, but disappointed by their time in Nevada. They had thought they were going to reconnect with their dad, but they found themselves with a complete stranger. They returned completely disillusioned. The three of us together spent the next year praying often before bedtime that God would change Daddy's heart and bring him home. A year later, I received another phone call from David; this time, he wanted to come home.

Coming Home

A month passed, and David showed up on my doorstep with all of his things, asking if he could reenter the kids' lives. He promised he would look for a job and find a place to live here in town while rebuilding his relationship with his kids. I wanted to help him out, so I let him stay at my place while I stayed at my best friend's house until he found other arrangements. I figured this would only last for a few weeks.

Six weeks later, no progress had been made—no job, no money, and no place to live. My best friend and her husband told me it was time for me to have some brave communication with David. Realizing they were right, I asked him to leave and find other living arrangements. This did not work out as I had planned. The kids, who were just starting to get to know their

What's Love Got to Do With It?

dad again, couldn't understand why I was asking him to leave. I, however, knew it was best for all of us that I come home and live in my own house. David needed to take responsibility for his own life and what he wanted to accomplish apart from me. He finally moved out, and we continued on with life as our family of three.

Several weeks later, I received yet another phone call. This time, David was asking about our relationship and whether or not we had a chance of getting back together; we decided to meet. That chilly fall evening is one that I will not soon forget. As I drove to the park where we were supposed to meet, I wondered, *What is going to happen? What is he going to say? How is this all going to work out?*

I pulled into the parking lot, trembling at the core of my being, but unsure what emotion I was experiencing—nerves? Excitement? Fear? It was just getting dark outside, and when David slid into the passenger side of my car, I could not see his face. I did not know what would come next. David began the conversation. "Do you think it's possible for us to ever reconcile?"

Completely surprised by his question, and a little bit excited, I responded, "Absolutely, I have been praying for that since you left."

"So what do we do next?" he asked.

I told him that, even though I had forgiven him, I needed him to prove to me that he had actually changed over a period of time. I suggested six months to a year. If that went well, I told him, "I believe we can start afresh."

David became a little agitated and proceeded to tell me that I was putting him in bondage because, if I had truly forgiven him, I would forget the past just like God does, casting our sins into the sea of forgetfulness.

I told him, "I am not God."

A little bit stunned, he said, "Then I guess you haven't truly forgiven me."

Within a month of that conversation, he began dating one of the girls from our former youth group, and three months later, they got married. I questioned myself, wondering whether I had made the right choice. *Should I have taken him back? Did I really forgive him?* I thought I had. Sadly, David's marriage lasted less than a year—which made me pretty certain that I had made the right decision. Once again, it was just the kids and me, and this time, I knew that David and I would never be together again.

My Pride and Joy

My kids were the love of my life. I poured my heart into them and tried, as best I could, to be both mom and dad for them. Initially, I was working in a doctor's office, but it did not pay me enough to raise my family, so I called my former boss and began working in road construction again. The hours were long and the work was hard, but my family was worth it. I had to be both the dad who brought in the money to meet the needs of the family and the mom who tried to meet the emotional and social needs of my kids. I did not receive any child support from David, so I had to do whatever I could to make ends meet.

What's Love Got to Do With It?

In the midst of all of this, some of David's family members, who couldn't have kids of their own, suggested to me that Michael and Christi should be taken away from me, that they should go live with them instead because (in their opinion) I could not raise them as well as they could. They had no idea what circumstances I had overcome, and I firmly replied, "No one will take my kids from me. No one can love them the way I love them." My message was clear, and my buddies and I continued life as a family of three.

Being a mom is the greatest thing in the world, though being a single mom may be the most difficult job on the planet. My kids were my pride and joy. I wanted to do everything that I could to make sure that they were happy and coping well, and I tried to fill the void created by the absence of their father. Obviously, this is an impossible feat, but I knew my kids did not deserve to be collateral damage from the fallout between David and me. I was determined to be the best mom I could possibly be, no matter the toll it took on me. However, during my life as a single parent, I often wondered, *Am I doing anything right? Should I have let David's relatives take the kids and raise them? Are my kids going to be a mess by the time they reach adulthood?* I spent many hours praying, "I really do not want my kids to be statistics. God, please help!" God had given me two very special gifts, and I had to trust that, as I did my best, He would give them His best.

As my kids grew up, they saw less and less of their dad. I came to terms with the fact that I would no longer see him or have him as part of my life, but I always wanted my kids to know their dad. I often protected, covered for, and made excuses for his absence. Once they got older, they sought to reconnect with their father and to rekindle what was lost in their adolescent years. When Christi was twenty, she decided that she wanted to move to Ohio, where her dad now lived, in order to spend time with him and his third wife, Tina, before she got married. This proved to be an important step for her and her dad, and the connection that came from that time was beneficial for Christi, enabling her to marry the man of her dreams without bitterness and resentment toward her earthly father.

The story was not the same for Michael. When he was seventeen, he decided that it was time for him to move to Ohio to get to know his father. Michael actually had a prophetic word from the Lord, saying, "You will leave Redding a boy and return from Ohio a man." This word brought him hope for his relationship with his dad. But a few months after he moved, David and Michael had a disagreement they could not resolve, so David asked Michael to leave. Michael spent the next year living on his own. He learned how to fend for himself, and in some ways, he did "become a man" before returning home to Redding.

I often wondered if things would have been so complicated had David really found the love of his life with the woman after me. He would have stayed close by, the kids would have experienced two families and life could have felt somewhat normal. We can't change the past, but I was willing to do anything for my kids.

What's Love Got to Do With It?

It was hard to let go and, at times, watch my kids walk into situations that would cause them more pain in their search for connection with their dad. Like all kids, they longed for the acceptance of their father, and they wanted him to impart his blessing to them. How could I say no to that?

The Single Life

I chose to remain single while my kids were growing up because I didn't believe anyone could love them the way I loved them. Although I dated a few times, I was very firm in my stance that I would not compromise for anything less than a man who could love and accept my children as if they were his own. During this season of singleness, I learned a great deal about trusting God to meet all of my needs. On many occasions, bills would be due, and I did not have the money to pay for them. Every time, without fail, the money came in. We always had the money to pay the rent and the bills, to buy food to eat, and to provide for the kids' school and sports needs. We never went without. God truly was "Jehovah Jireh"—God my provider—in those years. Like never before, I learned that my security, provision, and hope would always be found in the true Lover of my soul.

Though I knew remaining single was the best decision for my children, it created a deep loneliness in me. Often I would cry myself to sleep at night, just wanting to be held. One Sunday night after church, as the prayer team was praying for me, I went down under the power of the Holy Spirit and had an encounter with God. In the encounter, I saw myself standing before

Jesus. He had His hands held out toward me, and in the palm of His hands, I saw a human heart. It looked to be cracked, old, and sickly. He put one of His hands behind my back and pulled me close to Him, and as He did, He pressed the torn and tattered heart up against His chest. As He pulled me closer to Himself, the heart disappeared into His chest. As He stood there holding me, I began to feel my heart beat to the rhythm of His heartbeat. He whispered into my ear, "Let me be your husband." When I came out of that encounter, I was still lying on the floor, but I now had a diamond ring on my left-hand ring finger. At first I thought it wasn't real, but I could see it and feel it. I got up and ran back to my best friend, who had been watching the whole thing, and I asked, "Do you see it? Do you see it? Is it real?"

She said, "Yes, it's real. I saw the lady who put it on your finger."

This encounter happened in 1997. Fifteen years later, in 2011, I ran into the woman who gave me that ring at a women's conference. She had heard me give my testimony about that encounter at a women's group, but was never able to make contact with me. When we accidently ran into each other at the conference, she said, "I am the one who gave you that ring. It was a family heirloom." She was curious about what was going on in me during that encounter. I gladly told her, and then I asked her why she had given me such a beautiful diamond ring. She smiled and told me, "As I was walking by you lying on the ground, Jesus told me to go and

What's Love Got to Do With It?

put the ring on your left-hand ring finger because He wanted to betroth you to Himself. So I did."

Even to this day, when I feel loneliness at night or longing for a companion, the Lord reminds me of His love for me, wraps His loving arms around me, and holds me close. I literally feel His presence spooning me like a husband would his wife. His promise to be my husband has proven faithful, even on my most difficult days.

-Chapter 8-

Road to Destiny

When I decided to go back into traffic control for road construction, I knew it would bring in good money with benefits for Christi, Michael, and myself. I was a hard worker, and because this industry was truly a man's world, I had to work even harder just to prove that I could do it. Years before, I had worked traffic control when both of the kids were younger—just during the summer months to bring in a little extra cash. David had a friend who owned a traffic control company, and I was hired to be a flagger for a few local jobs. It turned out to be a good summer job because the kids were able to stay with close relatives, and they enjoyed hanging out with their cousins.

I only did this for a couple of summers when I was married, but after David left, when I contacted my former employer at the traffic control company, he hired me immediately. I worked for Traffic Solutions for the next eight years. I worked so hard that I was quickly promoted into a supervisory role and was able to land the closer jobs in town so that I could still be with my kids. I even worked the night shift for one year while attending Bethel School of Supernatural Ministry during the day. It was perhaps the most trying year of my life next to my divorce.

The Accident

The final year at my job ended tragically. The Lord had told me to quit my job a year earlier, but I was disobedient. I continued to work even though I wanted to do the second year at the Bethel Supernatural School of Ministry, because by that time I was making good money. I had worked myself into a pretty good position in the company, and I wasn't willing to leave.

But close to the end of the work season at Traffic Solutions, an accident happened that woke me up to the reality of where I was. I wasn't sitting in an air-conditioned office, a safe environment, or the fulfillment of my dreams. Instead, not only was I working myself to death, but the environment I was working in was extremely dangerous. The money was so good that I ignored all the warning signs—until one night in October.

Toward the beginning of a night shift one evening in late October 2005, after setting up a lane closure, I began making my rounds to make sure everything was safe. My job description was simple—keep the workers safe and keep the public safe. All of a sudden, a drunk driver blasted through traffic, heading straight toward the work zone.

What happened next was truly unbelievable. I had worked in that field for fourteen years and had never witnessed anything like it. One of the workers, Joe, a friend of mine whom I had gone to school with, was turning his piece of equipment around when the drunk driver hit him going about fifty miles per hour. Joe was not wearing his seatbelt, and upon impact, he was catapulted through the air and landed on the pavement just before the road sweeper he was previously driving, came crashing down on him; he was crushed from the waist down. In shock, the workers immediately rushed to help him. Pulling him out, they discovered that his complete lower body had been crushed. It was a horrible sight that sent me into hysterics. I thought, *This is all my fault! It's my job to keep everyone safe!* Before my very eyes, one of my coworkers had been crushed to death.

As we waited for the ambulance to arrive, I knelt beside Joe, praying and asking the Lord to spare his life. But I felt completely powerless, and when he died, I thought, *What kind of example are you, anyway? Not only did you slack on your job, but you can't even raise a man from the dead. Are you really a Christian? You are not only a poor employee, but you also do not carry the kingdom!* The lies I listened to that night plagued me for the next year and a half as I suffered from posttraumatic stress disorder.

The Lord now had my undivided attention. I am in no way insinuating that Joe's death was God's plan to get my attention or the result of my disobedience. I do believe, however, that He can use any situation to open our eyes to what He is saying. As I watched my colleague die, I realized that it could just as easily have been me under that machine and my children would

What's Love Got to Do With It?

have been left without a mother. It was at this point that I decided to get back on track.

Getting Back on Track

I enrolled in the second year program at Bethel School of Supernatural Ministry that next fall. The complete program is three years long, and since I had completed year 1 six years earlier, I was able to jump in to year 2 and get on track for completing the school. Because of the accident, I had quit road construction for good. I decided to dedicate that next year to pursuing God as a full-time student. *Who knows,* I thought. *Maybe it will somehow lead to a full-time ministry position at some point.* All I knew for sure was that my road construction career was over.

After I completed my second year, I asked if I could intern for one of the school pastors the following year. When I became an intern for Jason Vallotton, I realized that I had found my purpose in life. Never again would I stand on the roadway, feeling powerless and unable to save the life of someone who was fighting to live. Instead, I would fight for people to live life to their fullest potential, pouring myself into students so that they could become all that God created them to be.

As an intern, I was able to counsel, guide, and mentor students who were coming from all over the world. As I did, I came alive as never before. I began to fall in love with the students. And as I witnessed the students finding their purpose, I saw that they were coming alive too. I watched Jason lead his group, and I took careful notes on how it should be done. I absolutely loved how he poured into the lives of these very hungry and passionate people from every age group and every region of the world.

Before my one-year internship was even over, I asked if the school was looking for more pastors to hire for the upcoming year. After an interview, they offered me the job. Our church was no longer associated with the denomination that forbid divorced pastors, and so began my journey into the third major dream that I had set my heart on so many years before. Finally, it was becoming a reality!

To this day, I continue to live in the fulfillment of my dreams. Each year I have the privilege of loving and pouring hope into the lives of individuals who come to Redding from all different walks of life, age groups, and regions of the world. Before Christi and Michael moved out, I often wondered if the empty-nest syndrome would hit me like I heard it would. As a single parent, watching my kids spread their wings was not easy, but as I released my biological children from the nest, I gained the ability to spend my life pouring into spiritual kids as a pastor. I may no longer have children at home to care for, but every year, I meet a group of people who rapidly work themselves into my heart and become my "kids." I currently have over three hundred "kids" of all ages and from all parts of the world. And that number just continues to increase.

The revival that truly hit my little town of Redding, California, has stayed, and now Bethel Church is impacting the nations—and I get to be a part of it.

Part 2

Keys to Life in the Kingdom

-Introduction-

Building a Kingdom House

I have found my home in the center of God's love for me. I can follow the paths and directions that take me directly to Him, to the heart of my Father, who always has room for me. In this place, a kingdom house is being built so that my children and generations to come will forever have a place to call home. Jesus assured the disciples of this very thing:

Don't let your hearts be troubled. Trust in God and trust also in me. There is more than enough room in my Father's house. If this were not so, would I have told you that I am going to prepare a place for you? When everything is ready, I will come and get you, so that you will always be with me where I am. (John 14:1–3, NLT)

I always wanted to have a place to call home. As a child, in the midst of all the moving and changing locations, I longed for a place to go home to. I wanted roots. Now that I am older, I am realizing the importance of knowing where we come from and where we are going. In this awareness, we can often find our roots and the foundation of what makes us who we are. Not all who wander are lost.

What's Love Got to Do With It?

During the remainder of this book, as I map my path and explain the methods by which I found my way home, I seek not to build a formula or a set of rules and regulations. Each of us must find our own way into the kingdom houses that are designed for us. These chapters are a blueprint for my house with Papa. I want to share them with you so that the very pieces that have forged my dwelling place can be taken, altered, and built upon so that your house will be built upon the rock. Then, when the rains fall and the floods come, your house will not fall (Matt. 7:24–27).

Chapter 9

Heritage and Inheritance

Five years ago, some of my family members began researching the history of our family lineage on my father's side. I had always wondered who we are and where we came from, and I was pleasantly surprised when they discovered some interesting facts. I come from an American Indian tribe called the Nipmucs, a tribe that originated in the Washington DC area. We were a small tribe of around five hundred people originally.

The name *Nipmucs* means freshwater wanderers; apparently my ancestors moved around continuously in search of clean water. My paternal great-great-grandmother was a full-blooded Nipmuc. Interestingly enough, she married an African American man. This is a rare combination in our day, but was almost unheard of in theirs. Both American Indians and African Americans are extremely spiritual people, so suddenly I understood why I felt so at home when I walked in to that little Pentecostal church on Kidder Avenue when I was just eight years old.

Growing up, I loved watching Western movies, but I never saw the American Indians as savages. Most of

What's Love Got to Do With It?

the movies portrayed them as such, and the cowboys were the heroes who cleared the Indians from the land, making it safe for "civilized" people to live in. Not until years later, as an adult, did I realize that the cowboys had actually uprooted the American Indians' way of living, challenging their very existence when all they were trying to do was survive. However, all along, it had been my secret longing that the American Indians would beat the cowboys.

When I watched a video clip of Rosa Parks sitting on the front seat of that bus and refusing to move, I cheered. I could attribute those feelings to a strong sense of justice, which may be part of it, but I believe that my heritage, my very DNA, plays a major role in so many things in my life. Before I knew my heritage, I identified with both groups of people in the midst of a society marked by hatred and racism. My own family, who came from the same bloodline, often resisted integration. My grandfather was so ashamed of his heritage that he left his family in Ohio and never told anyone where he was from. This secret went with him to the grave. However, the secret was discovered when my cousin did her in-depth research about our lineage.

My cousin is one of several family members who have been trying to get our American Indian tribe federally recognized. The U.S. government requires solid proof of tribe membership; thus, a thorough investigation ensued. What she came upon was nothing short of miraculous to me because it answered so many of the questions I have had over the years.

What she uncovered was that my lineage includes several Wesleyan ministers and Baptist ministers from Ohio, both male and female. She also traced our family tree all the way back to a man no one in my family had heard of—Joseph of Arimathea. I had to explain to my family that our distant relative, my seventy-first great-grandpa, was the individual in the Bible who gave his tomb for Jesus to be buried in (Matt. 27:57–58). I was thrilled with this newly discovered information, and once again, it became so clear to me that I, indeed, have been passed a torch from previous generations, and that some of the great cloud of witnesses mentioned in Hebrews 11 are my bloodline family!

Inheritance

My pastor, Bill Johnson, and his son, Eric Johnson, recently released a great book titled *Momentum.1* It is about passing on a kingdom legacy to our children, and it emphasizes the importance of generational inheritance, which I wholeheartedly endorse. This means that my family members, generations ago, left a legacy for me to carry and continue on with. My grandparents and my parents didn't have to hand it down to me; I got to choose to take it up and run with what had been started in my family line many years ago.

My dad and mom were not sold-out believers when they met, but they met in church because both of them had praying mothers. I firmly believe that prayer is powerful, and both of my grandmothers spent hours on their knees interceding for their kids and grandkids. Though I was not raised in a Christian home, I lived under the covering of these amazing women. In Proverbs 13:22, it says, "A good man leaves an inheritance to his children's children." Because of the generations before me, I have a rich spiritual heritage to glean from.

Neither one of my parents gave their lives to the Lord until much later in life. My mom had asked Jesus into her heart when she was young, but did not follow the Lord after she met my dad. About seven years ago, just after my father was diagnosed with Alzheimer's disease, both he and my mom gave their hearts and lives to the Lord. This was the fulfillment of the prayers of my powerful grandmothers, who had long ago become a part of that great cloud of witnesses—prayers that I also began to voice when I accepted the Lord at the age of nine.

The flame that I now carry is not only the flame that my ancestors carried, but it was also part of the original flame of Pentecost (Acts 2). I am living in the inheritance of what my ancestors, as lovers and followers of Jesus, left for me. I am certainly not ashamed. Even though my grandfather was embarrassed by his family, I am grateful that truth prevailed and his secret was exposed so that I can run with this torch and pass it on to my children's children—never again to be extinguished.

A Mother's Love

I believe that my mother always loved the Lord; she is the strongest, bravest person I know. I watched unconditional love lived out right before my eyes in the person of my mother, who endured the harsh treatment of a strict, verbally and emotionally abusive husband. She waited on him hand and foot as, in her mind, a good wife should. He was the king of the castle, and she was his servant. She loved him through it all, and to this day, she would give her life for him. Many of my best character traits I get from her.

My mom valued her family above everything else. She defended my dad many times, she supported my brothers when they got into trouble at school, and she protected me from outside ridicule. She stood in opposition against any situation that threatened to harm our family. She also always encouraged my gifts. Often, I would sing simple songs to her that I had made up on the spot, and she would always laugh and smile and tell me how much she liked them. I always felt loved, believed in, and supported by her; I still do. She taught me what it looks like to be a mother. Truly, she is the epitome of the perfect mom and wife, and she loves well. I am pretty sure that my mom is a saint—the most amazing woman I have ever met.

Given the details of my childhood, my praise of her may surprise some. However, she didn't know what was happening to me. A few years ago, I told her about what my brother had done to me, and it broke her heart; she was truly devastated. I told her that I have forgiven him and that I also forgave her for not knowing or protecting me. I had moved on. But when I saw her reaction, I realized how deep her love for me ran. She would have done anything to protect me, and had she known, I know she would have come to my rescue.

As I think about my parents and grandparents, I am faced with the question, *What am I leaving to my children?* How can I repair the shattered pieces of their lives as children of a broken family, creating, in spite of it all, a powerful legacy for them? Better yet, *What am I leaving to my children's children?* This section of the book is dedicated to that very subject. I want my children, my children's children, and the generations that I will never meet this side of heaven to pick up where I leave off, to make my ceiling their floor, and to carry this message of the kingdom in a way that is unique to our family heritage. I want to build a house for them and pass on a legacy.

Chapter 10

The Presence

One of the most important things that I wish to pass on to future generations is a deep hunger for the presence of the Lord and an understanding of how to cultivate a lifestyle of worship. It is the very foundation on which I will begin to build this house. I live by a strong conviction that worship is not something we do or a set of songs we sing a couple times a week at a church service; rather, worship is who we are.

I began singing to my kids when they were still in my womb. As they grew up, they gained an appreciation for worship simply by observing me in my passionate pursuit of the Lover of my soul. Even in the tough times during the divorce, they watched as I continued to worship, and I began to notice them developing their own desire for the presence of the Lord.

On numerous occasions, I vividly recall watching my teenage son and daughter during worship services at church. Tears streamed down their faces, their heads and hands were lifted high, and their hearts reverently bowed low as they sincerely worshipped while Papa God enveloped them in His loving embrace. It was then that I realized they had been closely watching me, and I witnessed a torch being passed.

Worship is much more than singing; it takes on many forms in my own life. True intimacy with God comes from a life of worship, so it's important to understand not only what worship means to me, but what Papa God says about it as well.

The *Merriam-Webster Dictionary* gives many meanings for the word *worship;* some of my favorites are as follows:

To express praise and devotion; reverent honor and homage paid to God or any sacred person or object

To place in high regard as the object of adoring reverence

To turn and kiss

Worship in Spirit and in Truth

In John 4:21–24, Jesus declared,

> Believe me, a time is coming when you will worship the Father neither on this mountain nor in Jerusalem. You Samaritans worship what you do not know, we worship what we do know, for salvation is from the Jews. Yet a time is coming and has now come when the true worshipers will worship the Father in the Spirit and in truth, for they are the kind of worshipers the Father seeks. God is spirit, and his worshipers must worship in spirit and in truth.

The Samaritan woman was changed after her intimate encounter with Jesus. Her whole focus shifted from retrieving water from a well to being loved and transformed—something she had not been expecting. She then went back into her city, testified to people who did not think very highly of her, and transformed the atmosphere. She became worship because of her encounter with perfect love!

The following verses give an even-fuller picture of what worshiping in spirit and in truth looks like:

> Ascribe to the Lord the glory due his name. Bring an offering and come before him; worship the Lord in the splendor of his holiness. (1 Chronicles 16:29)

> Create in me a pure heart, O God, and renew a steadfast spirit within me. (Psalm 51:10)

> Come, let us bow down in worship, let us kneel before the LORD our Maker. (Psalm 95:6)

> Worship the LORD in the splendor of his holiness; tremble before him, all the earth. (Psalm 96:9)

> Exalt the LORD our God and worship at his footstool; he is holy. (Psalm 99:5)

> Worship the LORD with gladness; come before him with joyful songs. (Psalm 100:2)

From these passages, we can see that we were created to worship. We were created for worship; we were created to be worship. Worshiping anything other than the One who created us is not only idolatry, but is a perversion of who we are.

What's Love Got to Do With It?

The phrase *worshipping in truth* may seem ambiguous to some. However, *truth*, in the very sense of the word, means reality or actuality. Being our most authentic selves without false pretenses or performance is a vital aspect of kingdom living. Worshipping in anything other than truth is giving our Creator, Lover, and Father less than He deserves. We don't *do* worship; we *are* worship. If I try to perform or live someone else's life of worship, I am not worshipping in truth.

Live by the Spirit

In Galatians 5:16–18, Paul wrote,

> So I say, walk by the Spirit, and you will not gratify the desires of the flesh. For the flesh desires what is contrary to the Spirit, and the Spirit what is contrary to the flesh. They are in conflict with each other, so that you are not to do whatever you want. But if you are led by the Spirit, you are not under law.

When I wake up in the morning, my first thought is, *Good morning, Papa.* My first connection when I wake out of my unconscious state is with the Infinite One. All throughout my day, I cultivate an awareness of His presence by paying attention to the condition of my heart. If at any point during the day, I experience negative emotions that are seeking to steal my peace, then I know that I have not cultivated His presence. I take a step back, see where I lost my peace, take the needed steps to restore it, and continue to walk in love, joy, peace, patience, kindness, goodness, faithfulness, gentleness, and self-control (Gal. 5:22–23). When I find and continue to walk in the presence of God, then I am truly "living by the Spirit."

Continuously Be Filled by the Spirit

I have often heard Bill Johnson say, "Walk around as if the Holy Spirit were a dove on your shoulder." This reminds me of what the apostle Paul wrote to the Ephesians:

> Be very careful, then, how you live—not as unwise but as wise, making the most of every opportunity, because the days are evil. Therefore do not be foolish, but understand what the Lord's will is. Do not get drunk on wine, which leads to debauchery. Instead, be filled with the Spirit. (Ephesians 5:15–18)

Many things could be said about being filled by the Spirit, but for me, on a daily basis, this relates primarily in what I allow into my mind, spirit, soul, and body. I have the responsibility to protect what I allow into a realm of influence in these areas. This is not something that I do out of fear or anxiety, but because I desire to consecrate my life unto God. I get to choose what I expose myself to, including the images I watch on television or in movies, the music I listen to, the conversations that I have with people, the books that I read, and how I spend my time. All of these areas of influence in my life must be continually saturated with the Spirit. In addition to praying in the Spirit and asking for more of the Holy Spirit, I am constantly being filled by the Spirit through my choice to fill my life with things that honor Him.

A legacy of worship and pursuit of the presence of God is the very foundation on which to build this house. It is my desire that this house remain in the family, never to be sold or deserted. For that to happen, it needs to have a firm, solid foundation that will never crack or fail even in the strongest of earthquakes or storms.

Chapter 11

Daily Abiding

After building the firm foundation of worship and daily cultivating His presence, it is important to begin constructing solid walls that even the most severe infestation of termites are not able to penetrate. These walls are built by remaining hidden in the secret place.

Come To Me

Twenty-five years ago I had a dream that, to this day, impacts me deeply. I encountered the presence of God so strongly that when I awoke, I felt Him all around me. It went something like this.

Standing alone in the middle of a field, I stared up at an ancient English-style castle complete with a moat surrounding it. All around the castle was scaffolding, and it looked to be under renovation. As I walked up to it, a set of huge arched wooden doors opened before me. I pushed past them into a dark room. There were no lights and no windows, but even in the darkness, I could somehow see where to keep walking.

I forged ahead and came to another set of double doors identical to the first ones. As I pushed through this set of doors, I realized that it was a duplicate of the first room, darkness and all. I decided to continue walking, and I found myself standing in front of a third set of double doors, that I also pushed open.

The doors opened. A dense fog covered the ground, and the air was chilled with a cold moisture that surrounded me. This room, in contrast to the two previous ones, had a light coming from the far end of the room. From the same direction as the light, a warmth radiated my way. Out of nowhere, a voice said, "Sit down. Take off your socks and shoes."

As I was complying with this order, another one came. This time the voice said, "Come." I looked down and saw a grocery bag sitting beside me, so I picked it up and walked toward the warmth and light emanating from the corner. I was not instructed to pick up the grocery bag, but I did it anyway. At this point, I noticed that there were hundreds of people in the room, all headed in the same direction.

I had never seen these people before, but I knew they were kindred spirits, people who loved the Lord. I couldn't see their faces, but I knew they were church people. The chill in the room quickly became a blue-black cold, and all I could think about was escaping it by getting to the illumination at the far end of the room.

My journey continued, and I began to notice that, as long as I kept my eyes and path directed toward the light, I would be pulled and drawn with urgency. But when I turned my eyes away to see what everyone else was doing, I was gripped by fear. Surely, I thought, I must have missed a command because when I looked around, I noticed that all the other people were doing something that I was not doing. The other people in the room were all picking up socks and shoes and putting them in the bags that they were carrying. Scared that I missed an instruction, because the others in the room were doing something I was not doing, I began to cry and was overcome by fear to the point that I couldn't move.

Fortunately, the instant that I fixed my gaze on the corner of the room, where the light so brightly shone, nothing else mattered. The pull and draw of light and warmth returned, as did my goal. This cycle repeated itself three times, and each time I looked away, I noticed something different. The second time I looked at the other people, I noticed that they were dragging their bags. It seemed peculiar, but I still thought I had missed something. Upon the third glance, I noticed that many of them were so exhausted from the journey, with the bags that had become too heavy to carry, that they were sitting on the ground, unable to continue.

As I approached the fringes of the light and warmth, I was saturated in this deep love, revealing its identity—God. I dropped my bag and continued drawing closer into the presence within the light. An outline of a figure appeared in the light, sitting on a throne with a moat surrounding it. The only way to the figure was by crossing the moat via a narrow piece of wood.

Standing on the bank of the moat, I saw flames and snakes shooting up from it. Combined with the blood-curdling screams that resounded through my ears, I decided to look for another way because crossing that plank seemed impossible given my fear of heights and all the distractions. I had to find another way to the Lord, so I began circling the moat.

Revolving around the moat only intensified the fear. The snakes were more hideous, the flames ready to engulf me, and the screams more ear-piercing than before. After the third revolution, I looked and saw the feet of Jesus sitting on the throne. Instantly, the plank became a platform and I ran across. I turned to see if anyone was with me, and I saw one person standing next to me. Turning back to look at the Lord, I saw my hand reach out in an attempt to touch Him. I came within centimeters of His skin when I suddenly awoke from the dream.

When my consciousness returned, I could feel an infusion of love and peace; I knew the Lord was in the room. It was so intoxicating that I fought with all my might to go back to sleep so I could return to this dream. Much to my disappointment, I was unsuccessful.

I began to ask the Lord what all this meant. I knew that this was an encounter that I would remember forever, and I wanted a better understanding of what God was saying in the midst of it all. It has taken me years to fully understand it, and I have found refuge in this encounter on several different occasions when the Lord has brought it to my attention. Here is a brief interpretation of what I believe God was saying to me.

Castle—The castle represented my life. In the first phase of my childhood as a sickly child, it was dark and hopeless, but I survived. This survival led to the second room, which I identified with my abuse. It was in the third room, or third season of my life, that I found the Lord.

The Scaffolding—The scaffolding indicated that, although the castle looked completely constructed, it was in desperate need of renovation.

Socks and Shoes—The socks and shoes represented the cares of the world.

People in Room—These faceless people were those whom I had gone to church with, worshipped with, and served with in my years as a Christian.

Grocery Bag—The grocery bag is a container to put things in. I was not commanded to take it; that was a choice that I made all on my own. I was given the freedom to take it or leave it. It was ultimately used to carry burdens that I and the others were not instructed to pick up.

The Light—The bright, warm light at the far end of the room was the Lord Himself. His presence was beckoning to me with every step I took. Every time I allowed my eyes to move away from the light, I lost my focus. I became fully aware of my surroundings and was distracted by the activities of those around me. Because I lost my focus, fear gripped me.

The Number 3—I looked around three times, was distracted three times, passed through three sets of double doors, entered three rooms, and made three complete revolutions around the moat. The number 3 signifies the Trinity, and I believe the Lord was showing me that He was with me the whole time, even when it was cold and dark.

What's Love Got to Do With It?

All of these things were highly symbolic, and they helped me to know that God was and is with me. Perhaps the most significant revelation has to do with the person who made it across the bridge with me—my earthly father. My entire childhood, my dad claimed to be an agnostic. He actually first began to profess atheism and really was not sure about God's existence. He then moved on to being a relativist and thought that people should choose for themselves how to worship God without outside pressure. Many years later, when he was diagnosed with Alzheimer's disease, he gave his heart to the Lord. This dream provided assurance that Dad would indeed be in heaven with me.

The importance of this dream is that it represents a picture-perfect example of what we get when we abide daily in the Father's love. When we get distracted by the things of the world or shift our focus away from His face, we risk picking up burdens that we were never meant to carry and living in a place of fear and darkness. He is with us even in those places, but it is in the beauty of seeking His illuminating presence, basking in His warmth, walking in His safety, and dwelling in His unconditional love that we find His face.

Falling in love with the Lord on a daily basis and cultivating a consistent relationship with Him will create a solid structure that, once the house is complete, will be visible to all, and such a structure is necessary for the very stability of the house. Jesus warned the church in Ephesus, saying,

I know your works, your labor, your patience, and that you cannot bear those who are evil. And you have tested those who say they are apostles and are not, and have found them liars; and you have persevered and have patience, and have labored for My name's sake and have not become weary. Nevertheless I have this against you, that you have left your first love. Remember therefore from where you have fallen; repent and do the first works, or else I will come to you quickly and remove your lamp stand from its place—unless you repent. (Revelation 2:2–5, NKJV)

This warning clearly shows us the importance of cultivating our intimacy with the Lord as the foundation upon which we build the rest of our lives.

Falling in Love Daily

Being in full-time ministry, I am fully aware of the pitfalls of my position. If I am not falling in love with my Lord daily, I literally feel the pressure of my life sucking me into a vortex of "works" and draining me of my passion. Although everything I do is for the kingdom and it is all good stuff, if I am not careful to maintain my personal connection with my Lover, I slowly begin to slip away from my first love. This is dangerous because, in the midst of doing incredible things "for God," we can miss what God is actually calling us to do. Daily communing and connection with Papa God in the secret place is a non-negotiable in my life.

It is somewhat similar to falling in love in the natural. Let me explain. When I first fell in love with my husband, I was unable to function as a normal human being. That is the absolute truth! It was difficult for me to eat; I completely lost my appetite every time I would think of David, which was quite often. When I was not with him physically, I was daydreaming of him during my waking hours and having dreams about him while I was asleep; therefore, I had a tough time concentrating. When we would call each other on the phone and run out of things to talk about, we would just sit and listen to one another breathe. Just knowing that he was on the other end of the phone in my hand and hearing his breath come through it excited me! Is that normal? It is for someone who is experiencing a new love. Every time we had a chance to be together, we would make the most of it; we had no idea when we would next see each other since we both still lived at home, went to school, and lived under a curfew.

The analogy astounds me, and it makes perfect sense to me that the Lord would speak so highly of marriage. Paul wrote in his letter to the Ephesians:

> Husbands, love your wives, just as Christ also loved the church and gave Himself for her…So husbands ought to love their own wives as their own bodies; he who loves his wife loves himself. For no one ever hated his own flesh, but nourishes and cherishes it, just as the Lord does the church. For we are members of His body, of His flesh, and of His bones. For this reason a man shall leave his father and mother and be joined to his wife, and the two shall become one flesh.

> This is a great mystery, but I speak concerning Christ
> and the church. (Ephesians 5:25–32, NKJV)

The covenant relationship described in the Scriptures as a rewarding and holy experience called marriage is the same relationship that God wants us to have in union with Him. It is the perfect example of love. As in any kind of love relationship, it is vital to keep the fire burning by rekindling that first love experience daily. I cannot afford to allow familiarity to settle in, causing me to slip into performance mode and douse the flames of passionate love. If I do, I will slowly burn out.

Through the "loss" of my husband, who happened to be my first romantic love, I have come face-to-face with the reality that love of any kind must be fed daily or it will indeed die. It has caused me to value daily connection and spontaneity rather than ritual and form.

Atmosphere of Love

Over the years, I have closely observed couples who have been married for a long period of time. What I have noticed is that these couples actually begin to look like each other. My parents, who have been married for over fifty-eight years, are prime examples of this phenomenon; even their mannerisms are similar. If this is true in the natural, it is even truer in the supernatural. We begin to look like the One whose eyes we are intently gazing into. We take on His mannerisms—healing the sick, raising the dead, casting out demons, and releasing the captives.

What's Love Got to Do With It?

The practice of falling in love with my Papa, Jesus, and the Holy Spirit daily also creates an intimacy that literally shifts the atmosphere around me. The woman at the well absolutely fascinates me because she embodies this powerfully:

> A woman of Samaria came to draw water. Jesus said to her, "Give me a drink." For his disciples had gone away into the city to buy food. Then the woman of Samaria said to Him, "How is it that you, being a Jew, ask a drink from me, a Samaritan woman? For Jews have no dealings with Samaritans." Jesus answered and said to her, "If you knew the gift of God, and who it is who says to you, Give me a drink, you would have asked Him, and He would have given you living water." (John 4:7–10, NKJV)

As the story continues, we can see the results of an intimate encounter with Jesus, who truly expresses love to a person who had never experienced unconditional love. Jesus gently and lovingly spoke to a woman who was not only from the hated mixed race of Samaritans, but who lived a lifestyle that was not accepted by the general public, let alone by the church leaders. She was a scorned woman, retrieving water in the heat of the day so that she could avoid the criticisms and condescending glances of her counterparts.

Then she meets Love face-to-face in an interaction that drastically changed her life forever. In turn, she testified about this Living Water to the very ones who had chastised her. Through her encounter and subsequent witness, she shifted the atmosphere over an entire city simply because she had been touched by an intimate connection that she had never before experienced. That is intimacy at its finest! I wonder, did the woman simply forget to bring her water jug back to town? Or was she so in love that she was not acting "normal"?

What's Love Got to Do With It?

Chapter 12

Character

Now that the foundation is laid and the walls securely in place, the plumbing and the electrical must be properly installed in order for the house to be livable. Without running water and electricity, the modern house would not pass inspection and, therefore, could not be occupied. It may be a beautiful structure on the outside and pleasant to look at for the passerby, but if these things are not in proper operating order, upon closer observation, it will be apparent that the inside is unfit for comfortable living. It is merely a shell.

In order to continue dwelling in this kingdom and to pass on to my children a house that is complete with all the comforts of the kingdom, it is of utmost importance that my character be fully intact and in line with kingdom principles. Character is something personal and private that can only be seen by my Heavenly Daddy and me. In the same way, the important elements of a house can only be seen once the sheet rock is stripped away or the attic is investigated. Even the most important parts of the plumbing—the pipes and the septic tank—can only be seen after all the exterior elements, like the sinks and toilets are removed.

But if any of these are out of order, it is obvious to all the surrounding neighbors, especially if a septic tank is involved!

The Test of Blessing

Character can only be truly established and strengthened in a relationship of love and freedom. It cannot be built on rules, regulations, and religion. The challenge lies in the truth that when I live in freedom, where there are no "rules" to follow, I must rely on my intimate connection with the King in order to know His heart and to live in a way that pleases Him and brings Him glory and honor.

In Genesis 22:1–12, we read the story of Abraham offering up Isaac and being "tested" by God (see also Heb. 11:17–19). Is it possible that the very promise God gave to Abraham was a test? Abraham trusted God more than His promises, and He placed God's will above the long-awaited promise of many nations being birthed through his son Isaac. In other words, he never placed the value of the gift above the value of the Giver. He did not take his eyes off his Lover even if it meant returning his Lover's gift.

The children of Israel were also tested with blessing. In Deuteronomy 8:1–14, we read God's warnings:

> Every commandment which I command you today you must be careful to observe, that you may live and multiply, and go in and possess the land of which the LORD swore to your fathers. And you shall remember that the LORD your God led you all the way these forty

What's Love Got to Do With It?

years in the wilderness, to humble you and test you, to know what was in your heart, whether you would keep His commandments or not...For the LORD your God is bringing you into a good land, a land of brooks of water, of fountains and springs, that flow out of valleys and hills; a land of wheat and barley, of vines and fig trees and pomegranates, a land of olive oil and honey; a land in which you will eat bread without scarcity, in which you will lack nothing; a land whose stones are iron and out of whose hills you can dig copper.

When you have eaten and are full, then you shall bless the LORD your God for the good land which He has given you. Beware that you do not forget the LORD your God by not keeping His commandments, His judgments, and His statutes which I command you today, lest—when you have eaten and are full, and have built beautiful houses and dwell in them; and when your herds and your flocks multiply, and your silver and your gold are multiplied, and all that you have is multiplied; when your heart is lifted up, and you forget the LORD your God who brought you out of the land of Egypt, from the house of bondage. (NKJV)

The Israelites received abundant blessings. In return, God only made one request of them—that they not forget the Lord, but keep His commandments. They watched multiplication happen on every side, and unfortunately, they did not have the character to remain faithful in the midst of blessing. Blessings exaggerate what is in our hearts. If we have greed, jealousy, envy, or strife in our hearts, that will be exposed. In the same manner, if we have the character and nature of a life in the Spirit, then the fruits of the Sprit will be revealed in us. Blessing gives power and power exposes the heart.

Through any season of blessing, we are faced with the question of who is going to get the credit for the fruit in our lives. The Israelites never realized that God was blessing them because He loved them and considered them faithful. It wasn't a trick to get them to fail. He was simply giving them the opportunity to steward blessing well so that He could give them more. The test of blessing, when passed, brings more blessing and increase.

Taking the Long Way

My character was tested when I realized that I would have an opportunity to go from being an intern to being a pastor in the school of ministry. This is a highly sought-after position, one for which many people were more qualified and possibly even better trained for than me. It was because of the favor of God on my life that I was given this position, and I was eager to make the best of it.

In my first year on staff, I was faced with the difficult task of being entrusted with eighty-three lives in my revival group. Because the school is so large, the students are split into smaller groups called revival groups. My job is to pastor one of these revival groups during the first year of ministry school. I tried to run it my way instead of trusting God to lead me His way. This did not prove to be such a good plan, and it made for a really hard year. I focused on a bunch of rules, lessons, and teachings that were meant to be guidelines,

What's Love Got to Do With It?

and I focused the whole year on making sure that I did it right.

The following year, my son, Michael, said one day in passing, "Mom, this year you need to run your revival group differently. You need to just be you." This was all he said, having no idea about the inward struggle I had with leading my group. This changed the way I approached the revival group. I began to adopt them and train them as if they were my very own biological children. I was freed up to take the guidelines I was given and make the most of them in the midst of bringing all that I carry to my group. I may not have all the answers to all of their questions, and there may be problems I am not able to solve, but I could certainly love them. Because of these changes, my group saw tremendous breakthrough.

Each year is different, with a completely different mix of people, personalities, and needs. I have learned to ask God to lead me while I lead my group so that I have His plans and His thoughts for them instead of my own. He has never failed to give me everything that I need to serve Him and them well.

Tests and Trials

God tests with favor and blessing to build character, but our character also grows in the midst of hardship and trial. Many times throughout the Scripture, we see opportunities for growth in the area of character. One such story involves the disciples on the night Jesus was betrayed.

Jesus, having prayed this prayer, left with his disciples and crossed over the brook, Kidron, at a place where there was a garden. He and his disciples entered it. Judas, his betrayer, knew the place because Jesus and his disciples went there often. Judas led the way to the garden, and the Roman soldiers and police sent by the high priests and Pharisees followed. They arrived there with lanterns and torches and swords. Jesus, knowing by now everything that was coming down on him, went out and met them. He said, "Who are you after?" They answered, "Jesus the Nazarene." He said, "That's me." The soldiers recoiled, totally taken aback. Judas, his betrayer, stood out, like a sore thumb. Jesus asked again, "Who are you after?" They answered, "Jesus the Nazarene." "I told you," said Jesus, "that's me. I'm the one. So if it's me you're after, let these others go." (John 18:1–8. MSG)

In verse 10, Simon Peter took matters into his own hands and cut off the right ear of the chief priest's servant. On that night, the disciples were certainly tested in the midst of a major trial. They had given up everything to follow Jesus, and for three and a half years, they had faithfully followed Him, believing that the words He spoke were life and truth. They witnessed Jesus heal the sick, raise the dead, and set the captives free. Now, instead of feeling secure with Jesus, they were being threatened by a band of soldiers wielding weapons of harm, and the only thing their leader did was step forward and present Himself freely to His accusers without a defense.

These men had lived so intimately with Jesus for three and a half years, yet on the very night in which all of the Scriptures He had spoken about Himself would be fulfilled, they still didn't understand. I do not know what I would have done in that moment. But I do know that it is in moments like these where the test of our faith is actually a test of our character. This scenario with the disciples causes me to reflect on my own core value of trusting in God in the midst of trial and not trying to fix things myself.

Scared to Death

One of my most intense times of trusting God in the midst of trial, other than my divorce and the raising my kids, began at a BSSM staff meeting three weeks before school started in 2009. Mark Brookes, the BSSM first year overseer, began the meeting that hot summer day in much the same way he had done over the past twelve months. Halfway through the meeting, Mark asked us to pair up with other staff members and share our hearts on what we would like to see happen during this upcoming school year.

Mark paired up with me, and as he was sharing with me his heart, all of a sudden I was unable to see him fully even though he was sitting only three feet from me. As this was happening to my eyesight, my hearing also became muffled, and although I could see his mouth moving, I was not able to hear what he was saying. I became confused and scared, not knowing what was going on. I tried to formulate words to coincide with my thoughts, but as I would open my mouth, nothing would come out. As we sat there, trying to figure out what was happening, Mark asked me if I thought this was a spiritual attack. Because I am a healthy individual and had, just three days prior, completed a sixty-three–mile bike ride, I thought, *Yes, that is what is going on.* After I communicated as much, Mark asked the others to gather around me and pray. However, the confusion only worsened, so Mark and his wife, Rena, suggested we walk over to his office to call my doctor.

The next thing I remember, I woke up on the floor of Mark's office with two strangers in my face, asking me if I could hear them. I came to semi-consciousness and realized they were paramedics. In the background, I could see Barbara, one of my colleagues, with a concerned look in her eyes. I was in a complete state of confusion.

I spent the next seven days in the hospital, four of which were in the ICU, where they ran test after test in an attempt to find the problem. After a painful spinal tap, an angiogram, and every test in between, they found blood on my brain, but they were unable to determine why it was there. The next several months were filled with doctor appointments and further tests. The final conclusion was that I had suffered a stroke due to a disease they had found in my carotid arteries known as fibro-muscular dysplasia, for which there is no medical cure.

At the findings of this disease, I was warned to cut back on my physical activities since this could happen again without any forewarning. The doctors told

What's Love Got to Do With It?

me I might not survive the next time. I was to have a checkup twice a year until they could ascertain the situation. I was scared, really scared. This was not just a disease; it was a silent disease, void of symptoms, that would not give any kind of warning prior to a fatal episode. I began to pay attention to every headache, bit of confusion, or dizziness because what felt like a mild headache could actually be an aneurism. I was a prisoner in my own body.

The restriction on my physical activities only caused a determination in me to go after complete healing. I asked the Lord if He would heal me by my next checkup so that the test results would find absolutely no sign of the disease and I could resume my activities. I was careful, following the doctor's orders, but I was longing for the day when I could get back on my road bike and ride for one hundred miles.

In the midst of this very trying time, I learned how to completely trust that God had me in the palm of His hand. There was nothing that I could say or do to make the disease go away, but I could trust; I can always trust. I followed the doctor's orders by resting, cutting back on my physical activity, and paying attention to my body. It was a difficult season, especially because I was not able to work out or be as active as before. Simultaneously, I began to declare complete healing over my body, and I received constant prayer from others. I was a frequent flyer at the prayer line, knowing that I could be just one prayer away from complete healing. I was not praying or asking others for prayer so that God would do something for me; rather, I was praying from a place of assurance, knowing that Christ's blood had already paid for all sickness and disease. The people who were praying with me had this belief too, and we joined together and partnered with heaven for breakthrough.

Medical Miracle

I had been sitting in the little exam room for over an hour and a half, waiting for the doctor to return. I began to feel a little apprehensive, wondering what was taking so long; I later found out why. The doctor was sitting in his office pouring over the tests that had just been completed a week before, and he could find absolutely nothing wrong with me—no sign of any disease in my body! He told me that I was a medical mystery because I had no signs of suffering a stroke. In fact, the MRI showed that my brain was the size of a twenty-one-year-old! Thank You, Jesus! I am a miracle.

Three weeks before the start of the Bethel School of Supernatural Ministry 2011 school year, I rode one hundred miles on my road bike, a trip that took eight hours, nineteen minutes, and fifty-six seconds. I had no headache, no dizziness, and best of all, no stroke. I am now back to riding regularly, lifting weights, and working out. In fact, I am working out harder now than I did before it all began. God truly is in control.

This whole ordeal was perhaps one of the most difficult experiences of my life; it almost cost me my life. Now I am healed and get to look back on the situation and see how faithful God was in the midst of it. He truly stayed with me through it all and gave me the strength to endure no matter what the report. I set

What's Love Got to Do With It?

in my heart that nothing would separate me from the love of God, and this event was no exception. With my character intact and my inmost being kept pure, I am now able to come fully into the throne room and worship my King in spirit and in truth.

Chapter 13

Audience of One

The trusses are the part of the roof that cannot be seen; they are hidden from public view. However, they are an extremely important part of the house because without trusses there would be no roof. The trusses in this house are made up of the times when we perform only for an audience of One. These are the times in the hidden place with God when no one sees our "performance." In these times, we gain the ability to sustain all that we are called to walk in.

When I first began singing in church, I was told I had a gift. I really was not sure what that meant. I was eight years old, and I just knew that I loved singing. I would practice singing and preaching to my stuffed animals in my bedroom for hours on end because I loved performing and my imaginary friends were a captive audience. On one occasion, I imagined myself singing on stage in front of a large crowd wearing sparkly clothing much like Liberace, who was a famous piano player back then. He would come on stage in the most outrageous outfits that were covered in diamonds and play on his piano, which was also covered in sparkling sequins. His audiences were always captivated.

From a young age, I had believed I was a financial burden on my parents since I was in and out of the hospital so much. This was imbedded into my psyche even further when, as a child, my clothes were mainly purchased from a secondhand store—a fact for which I was often mocked by the kids at school. So in my playtime with my imaginary friends, I was sure to dress like the sparkly entertainer on stage who always won the approval of the audience. The performance that began in the solitude of my room, with my animals and imaginary friends, started to become a reality in front of people. As I progressed in my singing, I began to get a lot of attention for it, and many people thought I was on my way to one day being on the "big" stage.

My parents also noticed that I had a gift; they saw that I had passion too. My dad would watch me walk around with a tennis racket, which I held and played like a guitar. I would also draw a keyboard on a piece of paper and pretend like I was playing it. After a while, they made the decision to invest in voice and guitar lessons for me, and they even purchased me a guitar.

I would practice for hours on end and perform for my imaginary friends and all my stuffed animals. I loved the feeling I would get when I played even for that audience—an audience that I now recognize was not imaginary, but that consisted of the Holy Spirit and the angels. When the author of Hebrews wrote, "Don't forget to show hospitality to strangers, for some who have done this have entertained angels" (Heb. 13:2, NLT), he was probably not referring to my stuffed animals. However, it is comforting to know that, even as a child, I was learning how to enter into a secret place and perform only for my audience of One. When the time came for my first guitar recital, I was excited. I knew I was made to perform in front of people.

Made for the Stage

After my solo in the children's choir, which I mentioned in chapter 3, I quickly became more comfortable with singing in front of people. Performing for people truly made me come alive. It wasn't just about the attention that came as the result of being on stage; something in me shifted, and I felt like I became a different person. With each performance, I felt a connection to something bigger than myself stirring inside of me. I can't totally explain it, as it is different for every person, but using the gifts that we have been given for the glory of God brings about a change in us and in those we minister to.

In his first epistle, Peter wrote,

> God has given each of you a gift from His great variety of spiritual gifts. Use them well to serve one another. Do you have the gift of speaking? Then speak as though God Himself were speaking through you. Do you have the gift of helping others? Do it with all the strength and energy that God supplies. Then everything you do will bring glory to God through Christ Jesus. All glory and power to Him, forever and ever! Amen. (1 Peter 4:10–11, NLT)

Peter's advice is important for all of us because we all have a gift. When we direct our gifts in order to bring attention to ourselves, meet an unhealthy need, or bring glory to anything or anyone other than God, we make our gifts into idols. An idol is anything that takes the place of God or is set above Him in a position of priority over Him. We must be free from idols. Even the "good gifts" that Papa God freely gives to us as His children can become idols if we are not careful to always submit them back to Him.

I wholeheartedly believe that my Daddy in heaven was smiling, laughing, clapping, and crying with joy every time I used my gift. Even in the times when I performed for people instead of God, He was pleased with me, but my reward for stewarding my gift stopped with the praise of people. Now, however, I want a reward that lasts, one that will stand the test of time. Paul admonished the Galatians that they should be careful not to perform for the praise of people in anything they do (Gal. 1:10). When I realized that I often performed for the praise of people, I had to repent and dedicate my gifts back to God. He received every song, chorus, melody, and strum of the guitar strings with the heart of a loving Father, and that is the audience of One that matters.

One opportunity I was given to perform only for my Lord happened back when I was married and was one of the soloists in our hundred-voice choir. We were going through a tough time in our marriage, and David really did not care much about my involvement in the choir. It did, however, give me an outlet through which to use my gift of singing. When an opportunity to "try out" for a solo in one of the Sunday morning songs presented itself, I gladly jumped at the chance. I spent hours working on this piece because it was different from most of the songs that our predominately white, conservative choir had sung.

Our beloved director, Mark, was a man of high standards and excellence. He held a degree in music and was an exceptional piano player; at the time, he was also the associate pastor of our church. For months, we spent our Thursday nights practicing the same songs over and over again until they were ready to be performed for the congregation on a Sunday morning. This particular song that I was trying out for was a stretch, even for Mark. He had heard the song performed by the Brooklyn Tabernacle Choir and immediately felt the anointing of the Holy Spirit all over it.

He introduced the song to us via cassette tape on one of our rehearsal nights (this was way before CDs, but long after eight-tracks, so not quite prehistoric). As soon as he started the tape, the power of the Holy Spirit fell so thick that it felt like we were enveloped in a cloud of Papa's presence. We all began to worship the Lord in spontaneous praise—until two hours later we realized that we had not even practiced the song! Something was shifting in the atmosphere. Mark knew we needed to release that shift over the congregation and that this song would be instrumental.

Titled "In Everything Give Thanks," the song was a soulful piece, and since all of the members of our choir were white Northern California singers without formal training, it was, indeed, going to be a stretch for all of us. At that point in my life, I had not yet discovered that my great-grandfather was an African American. Had I known that fact about my heritage, I would have been better able to understand what happened next.

When I sang the solo in front of the choir for the first time, something happened in me that I had never

What's Love Got to Do With It?

experienced before. We were at rehearsal and working on several other songs when Mark announced that we would work on "In Everything Give Thanks" after we took a ten-minute break. Just the day before this rehearsal, Mark had called me and told me that I had landed the solo for this song. I instantly became nervous and began sweating. I literally thought I would pass out and totally forgot that I needed to use the restroom until it was too late. Not only was I nervous about singing, but I now feared I might experience the most embarrassing sort of "accident." Oblivious to all this, Mark handed me the microphone and announced to the choir that I would be singing the solo for this number.

As the music started, I noticed that I felt lightheaded. My body began quivering as though I was standing in sub-zero temperatures. As my hand tightly gripped the microphone, sweat began coursing through my pores, and the thought ran through my head, *After this, you will never sing again because you will fail so badly.* Immediately, I realized that the opposition of the enemy was trying to get me distracted, and I opened my mouth and released what would soon prove to be a new level of worship within our "conservative choir."

The presence of God hit me like a bolt of lightning, and I could not stand still. I sang and danced all over the room that night and released over the choir a freedom to move with the expression of abandoned love and adoration even in the midst of "practicing" a song. My soul was freed up to sing, and my body danced like David danced; I did it with all my might (2 Sam. 6:14).

Once the song was over, we again began spontaneously worshiping; it was truly amazing, and not only did something shift within me, but a transformation began to happen in the choir and our choir director. The next challenge for me, personally, came in presenting this to the congregation. I felt a freedom in the room that night, but I wondered whether there would be freedom on a Sunday morning with the entire leadership team sitting on the front row. Mark announced that we would be singing "In Everything Give Thanks" the following Sunday morning.

When Sunday rolled around, I felt as if a thousand butterflies resided in my tummy, and nausea was settling in. I wanted the Lord to show up and bless the people listening in the same way that He had lavished us that night in practice. I certainly had no control over that, but what I had experienced in my private times of rehearsing this song was nothing short of incredible. Each time I would go over the song in the privacy of my bedroom, the Holy Spirit would show up, and I would be on the floor in tears as I finished the song completely undone by the presence of the Lord. The cassette tape that the song was recorded on for me to practice with was totally worn-out, as were my vocal cords.

That morning, the choir gathered very early to pray and warm up. We all felt the power and presence of the Lord during our time of preparation, and the room seemed to buzz with excitement. We all felt something was, indeed, different on this holy day. All I was concerned about was the fact that I had rehearsed the song so much the night before that I had awakened barely able to talk, let alone sing. I never shared with anyone how nervous I was, and no one knew that my voice was strained and my vocal cords overworked. *How can I let*

What's Love Got to Do With It?

all of them down at this point? I thought. I had to completely rely on the Lord showing up because my voice was certainly not there!

As the first of two Sunday morning services began, we were all in our places on the risers on stage. Pastor Mark was the main worship leader at the time, and the one hundred-voice choir was his worship team. We had a small orchestra back then, and they were all in place as the congregation slowly began to arrive and settle down for a normal Sunday morning gathering at Bethel Church. Or so they thought.

A New Sound

We as a choir, the church, and the leadership team had been praying for the Holy Spirit to show up in our services in a tangible way. The fact that this song was being sung on a Sunday morning was pretty amazing; it was really more of a Sunday night number due to the freedom of worship that was allowed during that service. Although we wanted the Lord to show up, it had to be within our time limitations due to the fact that we had another large group of people coming in just two hours. And although we were a charismatic church, we believed our worship still needed to be done decently and in order.

When the morning celebration began, we collectively felt, as a choir, that this was not going to be the typical Sunday morning service. It began in the usual way, with one of the staff members welcoming the congregation as they entered, but even as this was happening, the choir was interceding. We knew what was about to take place with this song; after all, we had experienced its effects earlier in the week. I later found out this bit of information as we all discussed it in between the first and second service, but at the time, I thought I was the only one praying—which had absolutely nothing to do with being spiritual and everything to do with me being totally nervous.

I am not trying to gain any glory for what took place that Sunday morning. I did not feel anointed, and I was completely scared. I actually was operating in the fear of people and was performing once again for acceptance. I was so afraid that I was going to sing off key or forget the words. The memory of my first performance singing the solo as a child in the children's choir came rushing back into my head and taunted me about how I had made a spectacle of myself. I envisioned my friends laughing at me because, after finishing my solo, I had sat down on the front row and forgotten to finish the piece. On that Sunday morning, fear had the upper hand in my mind—that is, until the song began.

After we finished worship, which was charged that morning with a fresh wind of fire and passion, another staff member got up to make the announcements and receive the offering. I began to feel my vocal cords tightening in my throat, cutting off the oxygen to my brain so much that I thought I would pass out.

It came time for the song, and as the offering bags were being passed in the congregation, all of the people on stage were feeling a Holy Presence walk onto the platform. The music began, and I could tangibly feel the presence of the Holy Spirit overtake my entire body. It is difficult to express with mere words what took place over the next four minutes as the presence of the Lord

What's Love Got to Do With It?

literally walked off the stage and into the congregation. The power of God possessed me, and I began to dance down the steps, off the stage, and into the crowd. To my knowledge, this had never happened at Bethel before, and it certainly never had happened to me as an individual at a proper Sunday morning worship service. At one particular part in the solo, I remember sitting down on the front row, still singing, and making a point to those who were seated by AD-libbing, "And you think those people up there have it all together just because they are in the choir. They have to learn to worship in the midst of trial and 'In Everything Give Thanks.'"

I got up and began to dance throughout the sanctuary with all my might. By the end of the song, the people in the audience were all on their feet, and spontaneous praise had erupted much as it had with the choir members on our night of rehearsal! It was the first time I had ever experienced such passionate worship breaking out in a Sunday morning worship service. All I had done was be obedient to the call on my life, even in the midst of a personal situation that was extremely difficult. Through that, I learned a valuable lesson that Sunday morning. I learned to not fear people or failure; after all, what can people do to me? If I perform for the attention of people or for the affection and adoration of people, I fall extremely short of what I was created for—to bring pleasure to my Lover! He, in fact, is my audience of One.

The greenhouse for this lifestyle happens in the secret place. I cannot have a public ministry that has not first been cultivated in private. If I am not willing to sing for an audience of One, pour my heart out to God when no one else is listening, or write music that only He will get to hear, then I am missing the point altogether. The psalmist writes in Psalm 37:4, "Take delight in the LORD, and He will give you the desires of your heart." And Matthew reminds us that it is important to "Seek first his kingdom and his righteousness, and all these things will be given to you as well" (Matt. 6:33). My priority in ministry is unto God first and then unto the world.

It is, indeed, possible to see tremendous things happen on a corporate level simply because a person operates under the anointing or in his or her gift, but if we want to see true breakthrough and new levels in the Spirit, then we must take the time to create a history with God. This is not something that can be imparted or received from someone else. History with God is developed as a result of an intimate love relationship being nurtured and cared for over time.

Excellence Verses Performance

When we have developed a history, we will begin to see when we blur the lines between performance and excellence. Performance is carnal; excellence is kingdom. For everything that God created to be good, the enemy has made an attempt to distract and get God's people to believe a lie, by suggesting that a counterfeit is just as good as the real thing. By reeling people in with the bait of fame, fortune, popularity, position, or praise, he is able to hook them before they are even aware of the lure.

Several characteristics separate and delineate performance from excellence. Excellence is a condition of the heart; it is something that is implanted deep inside us by the Creator of the Universe that we are responsible

What's Love Got to Do With It?

for digging up and utilizing. Walking in excellence often requires a certain amount of sacrifice. Excellence does not search for the quickest way to a destination or a shortcut to make the journey easier. Those who walk in excellence always give their best without compromise, even when it is the most difficult and unpopular decision. Anyone can perform for something, and it can be difficult to discern performance from a pursuit for excellence. But only those who walk in excellence know the condition of their hearts and to whom they are giving their lives.

Excellence carries honor, but performance is marked by selfishness. When we live in excellence, we are not performing to be accepted and approved by God; rather, we know we already are accepted and approved. This enables us to live life out of a love *for* God and a desire to have relationship with Him simply because of who He is and who we are. We long to honor and please Him by being excellent in all we do, so we find ourselves serving God *from* love not *for* love.

What it all comes down to is an understanding and a desire to "keep the main thing the main thing." When we have our eyes fixed on an audience of One with the heart of a king or queen and the hands of a servant, we are right on track to bringing transformation to the spheres of influence all around us as we cultivate all we are called to walk in.

Chapter 14

Rest

Now that the trusses have been properly and carefully placed, the roof of this kingdom house can be confidently constructed. In my mind, the roof on the house I am passing on to my children is made of *rest*. This "kingdom house" that I am constructing must stand the test of time. It is a structure that I desire to keep in the family for many generations after I am gone. I want to be like the wise man who built his house on the rock.

> Therefore everyone who hears these words of mine and puts them into practice is like a wise man who built his house on the rock. The rain came down, the streams rose, and the winds blew and beat against that house; yet it did not fall because it had its foundation on the rock. But everyone who hears these words of mine and does not put them into practice is like a foolish man who built his house on sand. The rain came down, the streams rose, and the winds blew and beat against that house, and it fell with a great crash. (Matt 7:24–27)

These words were spoken by Jesus Himself. I cannot build anything less than what the Master Builder, who has designed the Master Plans, intends. As the psalm says, "Unless the Lord builds a house, the work of the builders is wasted. Unless the Lord protects a city, guarding it with sentries will do no good" (Ps. 127:1, NLT). The next verse says, "It is useless for you to work so hard from early morning until late at night, anxiously working for food to eat; for God gives rest to his loved ones" (Ps. 127:2, NLT). This verse does not give us permission to lie around on a couch all day, eating chips and bonbons and watching reruns of *Leave it to Beaver* while expecting the Lord to become our servant and provide for our every need. It is quite the opposite; the Lord desires to partner with us in every aspect of our lives, and that requires action on our part. I have just as much faith in the Lord providing for me while I work at my job as I do if I find myself unemployed. The Lord showed me when I was a second year student at Bethel School of Supernatural Ministry that *rest* is not a state of inactivity, but rather a state of mind and spirit.

Workaholics

When I was growing up, my dad taught me some profound work ethics. By today's standards, my dad would be considered a workaholic. I do not remember him being home much because he was always working two or three jobs in order to make ends meet. He started up his own trucking business when I was in my early teens, and he often told me that if he did not work, we would not eat. Now, being an adult and having raised my own children, I see this as an excuse for his absence in my formative years when I really needed him home to protect me and give me identity. However, in his defense, he was a good provider.

This set a standard in me that would soon prove to be a burden. Instead of allowing the Lord to provide, I felt it was my "Christian duty" to provide for my children by my own strength. Looking back on it all now, I see that, though I did not do anything that was a sin, I did not fully trust the Lord to provide for my kids and me. Instead, I began relying on my own two hands instead of placing my hands in the palm of Papa's hands and trusting Him to meet our needs.

I was not working when David first left, and within six weeks of him walking out the door, I had landed a part-time job at a local chiropractor's office. This chiropractor was a member of our church and knew that I had recently become a single mom. Though I had no experience in clerical work, he hired me, and I was extremely grateful for the opportunity. He and his wife trained me to run the front office, and I thought I was well on my way to a new career and financial stability. It felt like I had accomplished something pretty big—like I did not need David or his money after all. Little did I know that the pay for this job would barely put food on the table, let alone cover rent, utilities, and all the other bills that come with raising two very active teenagers.

After I received my first paycheck, reality began to settle in, and instead of trusting the Lord for His provision, I immediately began looking for a second job. Within two months I found another clerical position, but even between the two jobs, I was just barely

What's Love Got to Do With It?

making it from month to month. This continued for three months, until I was offered a position as a medical biller in a local doctors association. By this time, I felt pretty good about myself. Who needs a husband? I could raise my kids, work a full-time job, and still be a good mom—at least, that is what I thought. The truth is, I had begun trying to work all things together for my own good, by my own strength. But that was not my job at all (Rom. 8:28). It began to slowly take a toll on me.

I worked at the doctor's association for about a year and a half until I became bored with it. I began thinking of better ways to make money. I thought of my summer job years earlier as a flagger and remembered that the paychecks for one week at that job were the size of my current income for a month. I contemplated which of the two positions was the most appealing—sitting at a desk in front of a computer all day with a phone receiver in my hand or standing outside smiling and waving at strangers with a Stop/Slow sign in my hand. That's when I picked up the phone and called my former employer in road construction.

At each turn of my life, I stepped deeper and deeper into working myself into complete exhaustion. It happened so slowly that I did not even realize I had hit bottom until that fateful night at work when I watched my coworker die on a cold, dark street. It took so long for the Lord to get through to me because I was being stubborn and not resting in His presence. I was too busy for that; I had two kids to raise and a job that consumed about seventeen hours of my day, six days a week, for six months out of the year. During the winter months when I was laid off, I would catch up on sleep, which never really seemed to work. I could never catch up because I was physically, emotionally, and spiritually exhausted; I was a long way from rest. However, my bank account looked really solid, and I was able to give my kids everything they wanted—or was I?

Eventually, the truth began to sink in that I had become my dad. I had made a personal vow that I would never become like him, yet there I was living as a workaholic and telling my own kids, "If Mama does not work, you will not eat." *Sweet Jesus, help me!* I thought. Once I finally did quit working road construction and become a student, I soon discovered what rest really looked like in a practical way. Rest had so much more to do with a state of mind and spirit than I had realized. It was much more than simply sleep itself, even though I could sneak in a good nap at pretty much any location—including standing in line at the grocery store!

The Sabbath

Several times in the book of Exodus, the children of Israel were directly commanded by the Lord Himself to take the Sabbath day and rest (Exod. 20:8). They were even warned that if this command was broken, the guilty party should be put to death. I do not believe the Lord was so insecure and so desperately in need of attention from His admirers that He gave that command so that He would have complete and undistracted worship from His followers on one certain day. Rather, it is my conviction that the Lord, in all His grace and mercy, was setting up a guideline for us to not work ourselves to death! He Himself rested on the seventh day, and He is our greatest example (Gen. 2:2). So why had I thought I was able to work a full-time job, be a student, and be a single mom—and not need rest? It was my job, I thought. I had to do all of those things in order to be a good steward. I thought I would prove to David, his family, and all my critics that I was a strong, powerful woman who could do it all. To those closest to me, it was all too apparent that I was a very long way from resting in body, mind, and spirit.

Toward the end of my second year at BSSM, I encountered the Lord in a vision in a unique and significant way. I was waking up from a good night of sleep, and to this day, I am not sure if I encountered the Lord in a dream or an open vision. At any rate, I was lying on my side, and I felt a finger run down my side. Startled, I turned my head to see a very good-looking man with beautiful blue eyes, a stunning smile, and blond wavy hair that draped down to his shoulders. Looking down at me and smiling, He said, "Good morning! I have been waiting for you." He then reached out His hand, prompting me to take a hold of it, as if he were about to take me somewhere.

I grabbed hold of His outstretched hand, and instantly we were in some majestic place that I can only describe as heavenly. It was peaceful and vibrant with life. I was not able to see everything clearly, but in the splendor of it all, I was captivated by a very beautiful man who appeared to be in His mid-thirties with brown wavy hair that reached His shoulders. He had the most stunning brown eyes I had ever seen that enticed me to come closer. He motioned with His hand for me to come to Him. The closer I got to Him, the more I realized that I had been beckoned by my Lover, Jesus. The good-looking gentleman who had awakened me was still by my side, holding my arm, and we both walked over to Jesus. When we reached Jesus, I looked over to my companion to thank Him for leading me to this place, and I realized that He was the Holy Spirit.

The three of us walked arm-in-arm to a set of white stairs. At the very top of these brilliant stairs was a large throne. On this throne sat Papa God. My two companions and I began the ascent and approached this massive seat. The closer we got to the top of the stairs, the more I began to shake and tremble. I glanced over to my left and then to my right, looking for some sort of reassurance. Jesus and the Holy Spirit then gently lifted me up and placed me in the outstretched arms of a loving Father, who was simultaneously reaching out to receive me. Even though I was an adult, when I was placed in Papa's arms, I became a child.

Papa lovingly took me in His arms and held me in the same way that I would cradle my own kids when I was rocking them to sleep as infants. As I felt the warmth and safety of my surroundings and relished His strong embrace, I realized I was no longer trembling. I looked up into the most gentle and loving face, a face that brought me even more comfort. I settled into His arms. I was enraptured by His eyes—the most beautiful blue eyes I had ever seen—but I noticed that my Daddy was crying. Tears were falling from His eyes and

What's Love Got to Do With It?

landing gently on my face. I thought maybe I had done something wrong, but Papa assured me that they were tears of joy. He proceeded to tell me, "I have been waiting for you to come and rest in my lap." It was then that I realized just how tired and worn-out I had become.

Tears of sheer joy, yet utter exhaustion, began coursing down my cheeks, and I said, "How come I have never been here before?"

He replied, "You have been too busy."

"Daddy," I said. "I am so sorry that I have overworked myself and have come to this place of complete physical, mental, and spiritual delirium. Please do not let me go."

Then He told me a truth that will remain with me forever. He said, "Rest is not a state of inactivity. It is a state of mind, and you never have to leave." That encounter happened over six years ago, yet it is still impacting me to this day.

Choosing Rest

In my job as a staff pastor, it is very possible for me to run myself into the ground, and given my upbringing and history, I lean toward being a workaholic. Even though I am doing the very job that I long ago desired and that the Lord Himself ordained, I am still in danger of losing connection with my Lover if I do not remain in this rest of God. The hectic schedule, the meetings, the fast pace of my position, and the genuine concern for my students could completely destroy my kingdom house. If my mind, body, and spirit are not operating from a place of rest, my carefully constructed house will rapidly develop holes in its roof, and it will not survive the rain or the storms when they come.

How I personally cultivate a daily awareness with the presence of the Lord is very simple. He is my Husband, and each morning when I awake, I say, "Good morning, Lord" even though I am not able to see Him in physical form the way I did when I was married and woke up next to David. (Morning breath is certainly not an issue!) As I go about preparing for my day, I am continuously including the Lord in conversation. It almost sounds as if I am talking to myself or one of my imaginary friends, like I did as a child. He is there with me as I put on my makeup and do my hair.

Just before I leave my house I look in the mirror and say, "What do you think, Papa, am I ready for this day?"

In response, I feel Him smiling and saying to me, "You are ready!"

Sometimes He tells me to wait just another minute or two. When He does, I simply sit down on the couch and wait. I even have conversations with Him on my drive to work, and I cannot help but wonder what other drivers must think. Once I get to my office, I close the door, set my things down, pick up my guitar, and invite the Holy Spirit to join me. Sometimes I only have time for one song, at other times, I do not even make it through an entire song. It is not the amount of time that matters; it is the condition of my heart. I am simply allowing myself to become aware of His presence.

I realize this is not possible for everyone to do each day; in fact, there are some days when I am running late and do not get a chance to worship in my office at

What's Love Got to Do With It?

all. Again, it is simply a matter of being aware of Papa's presence all throughout the day. Recently, more and more people have picked up an amazing little habit that some have called the Ten-Minute Worship Revolution. These people attach a hidden buzzer to their attire— a buzzer that vibrates every ten minutes as a gentle reminder to give thanks to the Lord. One of my coworkers recently set her phone to vibrate every ten minutes to remind her to take a minute and remember all that she is thankful for and to worship in the midst of whatever she is doing.

I notice an obvious difference between the days when I do not make time for the Lord and the days that follow the pattern I just described. The days when I am in such a rush that I do not include the Lord are filled with anxiety and stress. By the end of one of those days, I am exhausted, and I come home feeling a little beat up. When I come home from a day of cultivating His presence, I come home refreshed. This further proves to me that rest in the Lord has everything to do with the condition of my heart and very little to do with the activity of my body.

Chapter 15

Lean on Me

The time has now come for the doors and windows to be hung in my house. The front door and windows of this kingdom dwelling are vulnerability. By *vulnerability*, I mean allowing others into my life to challenge me, strengthen me, and hold me accountable. Community cannot happen without vulnerability, and likewise, vulnerability cannot be effective outside of community.

Proverbs 27:9–10 says,

> Perfume and incense bring joy to the heart, and the pleasantness of a friend springs from their heartfelt advice. Do not forsake your friend or a friend of your family, and do not go to your relative's house when disaster strikes you—better a neighbor nearby than a relative far away.

In the first part of this book, I shared with you how I had to take a risk and begin to trust people after my husband left me for another woman and my church family left me for another church. At that point, I was able to reconstruct my house after the storm of destruction had left it all but completely leveled. Letting others into my life felt like a true threat immediately after

153 |

David left and my friends began to slowly move on to other churches. It seemed much easier to keep people at arm's length; that way I could protect myself. I was not too concerned about what people thought of me, and for a season, I did not let anyone into my life. My kids were my life for the most part, and my world was built around them. The only other people I had connection with were my parents and my best friend, Janese.

Best of Friends

Janese and her husband, Steve, were good friends with David and me when we were married. All four of us played on the church softball team. Janese and I played on the women's team, and Steve and David played on the men's team. Our kids would play together as well. Our son, Michael, and their son, Cory, were only two days apart in age. Our daughter, Christi, is about ten years older than Cara, Steve and Janese's daughter, but Cara looked up to Christi and somewhat idolized her. I do not know what I would have done without my beloved Janese and her husband Steve.

After the divorce, Steve and Janese adopted our little threesome and took us in as a part of their family. At one point, we even moved in with them and stayed for almost a year. They were and still are a huge blessing to my children and me. They helped me in every way to get back on my feet, and I thank God nearly every day for the role they have played in my life. It is because of them that I made it through the most difficult season of my life.

Janese stood by me, but she also knew how to draw the best out of me. She would constantly remind me that I had a call on my life to be in full-time church ministry. At times I would get angry with her and try to prove her wrong. "After all," I would yell at her, "I am damaged goods. How can I possibly have a ministry? Who would ever listen to a D-I-V-O-R-C-E-D woman?"

She would let me vent for a while, but when she got tired of hearing me gripe and complain and got fed up with my victim mentality, she would yell back, "I just wish you could see what God and I see! We certainly do not see some pathetic, washed-up, good-for-nothing old lady. So get up, brush yourself off, and get going. You have a job to do!"

My dear friends did not let me get away with self-pity or a victim mentality. She and Steve believed in me so much that they even paid for my school tuition. They are true friends, and they were willing to put their money on me, even if I would not have put it on myself. After all my years of praying for a sister, God had brought me one right when I needed her the most. Not only did Janese and Steve help me financially, but they also provided a strong support system for Christi and Michael. In fact, our families became so close that my kids call them Aunt Janese and Uncle Steve, and their kids refer to me as their Aunt Sheri. The Lover of my soul sure knew what He was doing the day He introduced me to Janese.

As close as we were, I still found it hard to totally let them in and trust them. Steve and Janese knew just about everything there was to know about me, yet I still felt that at some point they would leave me like the others had. They lovingly supported me through my worst times and my best times, and to this day, they have never shown me anything other than love. Yet distance came between us, in my heart, because of a lie I believed: "They will leave me just like everyone else did." In all reality, they very well could have left me; I am not their biological family, and they had no obligations to meet my needs. I was given the choice to take a calculated risk.

Vulnerability will always require risk. It doesn't matter whether you are going through the darkest season of your life and divulge a secret that could forever change a relationship with a friend or whether you are just calling a friend to see how he or she is doing; it will always come with risk. At least once every day, we are faced with the question that spans every culture and people group, "How are you?" Without thinking, most of us can give the standard answer, "Fine," or maybe, "Good." So what happens on a day when you are not fine or good? This is where risk comes in, and vulnerability can be cultivated. Each time you may choose differently, but ultimately, vulnerability is a choice.

I finally decided to make the choice with Steve and Janese and to be vulnerable to the max. They saw the good, bad, ugly, and everything in between. This felt like such a huge risk at the time, but it proved to me that I was truly worth getting to know and that I was even worth fighting for. Steve and Janese have shown me what vulnerability in community really looks like. Through them I have learned the valuable lesson of learning to lean on others and their continued love and support, which opened the door for me to begin to let others in. It is no longer as scary as I once thought.

It is not always easy to expose your heart, emotions, mind, or will to other people, but every human being is wired to desire connection. We were designed that way by the greatest connector of them all—God. He is the One who came in human form, bore His entire life as a testimony to the goodness of God, and then died completely vulnerable and exposed on the cross. Some people love Him and others hate Him, but the very thing that He died for, connection with the Father, required that kind of sacrifice. When we open up to others and make ourselves vulnerable, we are giving God a place to come in the midst of our community and create true connection.

The message of the popular song "Lean on Me" carries substantial weight in the reality of our lives. If I did not have my friends to lean on, I am not sure where I would be today. Being vulnerable and real with my close friends and family has allowed me to trust in humankind again. They have given me a safe place to go through life—the good, the bad, and the ugly—and still be accepted for who I am. Vulnerability gives me the courage to continue on and to fight the good fight, all the while knowing that we are fighting alongside one another and picking one another up. I now realize that I am my brother's keeper (Gen. 4).

Through Steve and Janese's example of accepting me for who I am, I now am able to love others into being who they were created to be. I was shown

What's Love Got to Do With It?

firsthand through love and sacrificial giving that it is possible to be vulnerable and to care for others in a way that releases the kingdom. This extends into all realms of our lives.

Brave Communication

When I was first hired as a staff pastor, I had to share an office with one of the other pastors. Since I had been away from the school of ministry for six years and since there is such an influx of students each year, I had never met Crystal Stiles. When we were introduced, I instantly liked her. In fact, the same year that I was hired, three other new pastors were hired as well, and we were all told that we would be sharing offices due to limited space. Inwardly, I was praying that I would be office mates with Crystal because I felt drawn to her even though I did not know her. I would soon find out that she has a passion for prayer and intercession, which coincides nicely with my passion for praise and worship.

Crystal is a true blessing to have as a friend, and she is not shy about speaking what is on her mind. I love that confrontation is not something she runs from; it is a quality in her that I truly admire because I strongly dislike confrontation. On one particular day, she saw that I was having a tough time with the way another staff member was treating me. I was not accustomed to telling anyone the inward struggles facing me because I had learned to deal with problems all on my own. She looked at me, gently closed our office door, and asked, "Do you want to talk about this?" I was totally shocked that she even noticed, let alone would address it with me. She then proceeded to tell me, "You should really pray about confronting this and not letting it slide." After talking with her, I did confront the situation, and it all worked out great. Crystal taught me a valuable lesson in being vulnerable daily with those I work with, and now, although it is still not my favorite thing to do, I will confront when necessary, and I love continuously.

Vulnerability gives a place for healthy confrontation to happen. When people do not feel like they are known, they often build a chasm between them and the world to keep others from hurting them. Vulnerability is what bridges the chasm. It brings people close and allows them the opportunity to see into me. When people really know me, I feel more comfortable confronting them because we have a relationship that I have invested in. But if I keep people at a distance, I give myself an out anytime a problem arises, and I am never forced to deal with it. Through vulnerability, we are known and we know others, which in turn gives us responsibility to develop our relationships through process. Trust me, the process is not always easy, but it is worth it. Vulnerability is always worth it.

What's Love Got to Do With It?

Chapter 16

Servanthood

The final door to be hung in my house is the back door, which I like to describe as serving the kingdom or serving others. The fact that it is the final door does not mean that it is least important; rather, I would believe servanthood is one of the most important aspects of kingdom living. It is impossible to imitate Jesus apart from being a servant. It is our ultimate goal and privilege to serve Him and one another.

In 1 Corinthians 12:14, we read that the body is made up of many parts. In verse 15, Paul writes, "If the foot should say, 'Because I am not a hand, I do not belong to the body,' it would not for that reason stop being part of the body" (1 Cor. 12:15). The passage goes on to emphasize that each part plays an intricate role in the healthy functioning of the entire body. I had to learn what my part was and be happy to serve the rest of the body in my role with excellence.

Upside-Down Kingdom

Service truly is the back door to the throne room. This might seem backward or out of order, but we live in an upside-down kingdom. Jesus said that the person who is the least in the kingdom will be the greatest and that the last shall be the first (Luke 9:48, Matt. 19:30). When we serve the vision of someone else, we get an opportunity to build a selfless kingdom. It is easy to have our own dreams and desire for what we want to build, but it is entirely different to choose to lay down our dreams for a season and serve someone else. What we will find, when we do this, is that when we take our own dreams back up again, we will have gained so much more insight and depth for our own vision—all because we took the heart of a servant.

Jesus was the ultimate example of a servant. As Paul wrote in Philippians 2:5–9:

> In your relationships with one another, have the same mindset as Christ Jesus: who, being the very nature God, did not consider equality with God something to be used to his own advantage; rather, he made himself nothing by taking the very nature of a servant, being made in human likeness. Being found in appearance as a man, he humbled himself by becoming obedient to death—even death on a cross. Therefore God, exalted him to the highest place, and gave him the name that is above every name.

If we are able, even in the smallest sense, to identify with the sufferings of Jesus, we will understand what true servanthood looks like. It looks like going low to see someone else exalted, even if we feel like we should be exalted. It could also look like seeing the value in what other people have to offer and serving them with our

What's Love Got to Do With It?

whole hearts. Jesus served even His enemies because love serves. Love gives, love sacrifices, love always looks like something. He gave His life for the sake of others, and He restrained His strengths and abilities in order to fulfill a covenant promise to all of humanity. He is the ultimate picture of selfless service.

Selfless service does not mean that we have to be doormats for people, and a true servant's heart does not operate in false humility. Kings and queens only serve when they choose to. They have people assigned to serve them all day long, but when they choose to do something charitable or for the good of the people, it is because they want to, not because they have to. True service is not an obligation; in fact, when it becomes one, the heart of the message has been lost. We don't have to serve; we get to serve. We get to lay down our lives to see the kingdom advanced. Service is not exclusive to the Church. We are called to bring the kingdom everywhere we go. True service can be even more powerful outside the walls of the church.

Serving Strangers

It has always been difficult for me to approach strangers, but when I feel led by the Holy Spirit, it is a bit easier. Still, it is a stretch. Once, when I was working road construction, I was setting up a lane closure in town. Basically, I was closing a lane so that work could safely take place. It is a difficult and dangerous job because I would have to set up signs and cones in live traffic. Being a bit exhausted, I went to my truck to take a short break before going to check the closure to make sure it was still safe.

The last thing on my mind at that point was the possibility of ministering to a complete stranger. I was getting out of my truck when I noticed a woman who appeared to be in her mid-fifties pacing back and forth on the sidewalk. Amused by her strange behavior, I watched her for a few minutes and noticed that she was barefoot. I found this a bit troubling since it was the middle of summer, and summers in Redding are not forgiving with highs over 100 degrees Fahrenheit. She continued walking back and forth, talking to herself, and making strange movements.

A little confused, I asked the Lord if He wanted me to say something to her. He said yes. So I walked over to her without a clue as to what I was going to say. My heart was beating out of my chest as I approached her. However, I also started feeling a deep sense of grief in my heart as I got closer to her. Her face was full of tears, so I asked her, "Is there anything I can help you with?"

She acted a bit startled and said, "Oh, I didn't know anyone was around."

I told her, "I have been watching you from across the street, and I noticed that you don't have any shoes on your feet."

She replied, "I was robbed last night."

She went on to tell me that she had been living on the streets for the last week. The mission did not have any beds available, and she had already stayed her full amount of allotted days. She then asked me if I was an angel. I laughed and replied, "Far from it." I asked her if she would sit on the grass and talk with me, but she hesitated, seeming frightened. I offered to get her a pair of shoes and asked her the size she wore. She was a size 8, like me. This prompted me to call my friend and ask her to bring me a pair of shoes that I knew my friend had just purchased.

While we were waiting for the shoes, I asked her if she was hungry. There was a restaurant close by, so I went and got her a hamburger. When I brought it back, I found her exactly as I had left her. Again she looked up at me and asked, "Are you an angel?"

I smiled once more and replied, "Absolutely not."

She said, "The reason I asked is because right before you got to me, I was in deep conversation with God. I asked Him what I am going to do. My money was stolen, I have no shoes and no food, and I want to get back to see my daughter, but now my money is all gone."

I listened patiently as she told me this story, and I felt a nudging from the Holy Spirit to purchase her a bus ticket to go see her daughter in Phoenix. About this time, my friend arrived with the shoes. We both offered to pray with her, and then we drove to the bus station. I purchased her ticket and watched her get on the bus. With tears running down her face, she said, "I am pretty sure you are an angel." She entered the bus, and I never saw her again.

The Lord taught me a big lesson that day. I could have passed this woman off for just another crazy person who was probably on drugs and was making up a story to get money and help, but the Lord stirred my heart with deep compassion for her. The outward appearances did not even come close to telling the true condition of this woman's life. She was truly in need, and my pity was not what God was asking for. God was asking me to serve this woman with my time, care, attention, and money. She did not need me to tell her how sorry I was for her; she needed me to love her. Love always looks like something. Serving this woman was a special experience that I will never forget.

Serving Another's Vision

On several occasions, I have seen God show up in the most random environments and display His love for people simply because I chose to say yes to the call to serve. Though service can happen in dramatic storybook fashion, it is not always something that looks life-changing. Don't let appearances fool you; even the smallest of decisions to say yes to service is life-changing.

At Bethel School of Supernatural Ministry, we serve not only the radical revivalists coming to our school to be trained up, but we also serve the vision of the fathers of this house—Pastors Bill and Beni Johnson, Kris and Kathy Vallotton, Danny and Sheri Silk, Eric and Candace Johnson, and many others. Though the many leaders and teachers in this house have varying messages and focuses, their overarching goal is the same—to see heaven invade earth! As staff and church members, we get to come under them and promote the Gospel of the Kingdom in every realm of society. As a result, we are seeing the nations of the earth flood our city, giving us an even greater opportunity—an opportunity to serve them!

Being a staff pastor presents some unique challenges in the area of service. I am one of fifteen pastors in our first year program, and I pastor a group of sixty to sixty-five students each year. These students come in from all over the world, and it is my job to help them through the different hurdles that come up during the school year. The hurdles are wide and varied, and all of them need to be traversed. I do not solve problems for students, which at times might be a little easier; instead, I solve problems with them. I get to serve them through the roller coaster journey that is first year.

Since we currently have around 920 students in first year alone, it is easy for our students to feel lost in the crowd. As I mentioned previously, to help them feel more connected, we divide them into smaller groups—revival groups. When school first begins in September, it can be a little intimidating for the new student to walk into such a large classroom, and often they feel somewhat overwhelmed. We as a staff do our best to make the students feel welcome, and on registration day, we are all set up to greet each of our incoming revivalists (as we call them) face-to-face. The desire that I had years ago to be in full-time church ministry sprang from my love of serving people, and my current position as a revival group pastor certainly fills that longing.

Nearly every day as I drive to work, I thank God for this opportunity that He has so richly blessed me with. We have a road known as the Avenue of Nations, and flags from each country that we serve line both sides of the street. Each day as I drive up this hill, I am reminded that it truly is an honor to host the nations, to train up these incredibly hungry-for-more-of-the-Lord leaders, and to send them out into the world. I certainly become attached to them, and as each graduation day approaches, I experience a range of bittersweet emotions.

The students we train are not only of varying ages (between eighteen and eighty), but they also come from many different backgrounds and carry unique life stories. When they land at the doors of Bethel Church, each one is just a face in a crowd of radical, passionate people. It is my job to care for them and love on them, to make them feel like they are known and like they are family. This presents a challenge because, in reality, we are all complete strangers. This is where I come in and serve. It is important to me that all of my students feel as if they belong.

The process of assigning people to one of our fifteen pastors looks something like this: The potential student fills out an application and sends it in to Bethel School of Supernatural Ministry, along with two personal references and one pastoral recommendation. The applicant then goes online to set up an interview. When I am given my interview schedule, I go over each of the names on my list before the day begins and pray over them. It is extremely important to me that I hear from the Lord concerning each person I interview. This is a huge life decision for the people coming, and I am only interested in serving those whom God has called

What's Love Got to Do With It?

to be here. The intensity of this first year program is not for the faint of heart.

During the thirty- to forty-five–minute interview, I am constantly praying. Once the interview is over, I usually have a pretty good idea as to whether or not this particular person is a good candidate for our school. It is my personal belief that everyone should come to at least the first year program, but not everyone is quite ready. After the interview, I pass on all of the information I gathered, including my personal notes from the interview, to our review panel. The review panel makes the final decision, and the applicant is then informed of that choice. Once the applicant has been informed that he or she has been accepted, a congratulations letter is sent. At this point, the soon-to-be student is placed into the care of one of the fifteen pastors. Once I receive my list of names and their pictures, I immediately print it out and begin praying over them. I ask the Holy Spirit to show me how I can best serve them in the upcoming year. Though it takes many forms, essentially, I best serve my students through love.

Finding a Place

Within the first week of school, I get the opportunity to introduce myself to my new revival group family. Most of my students do not know how to take me at first because I let each of them know just how important they are to me and that I love them. Their typical response usually is, "How can she say she loves me? She doesn't even know me!" As the year progresses, they begin to see me walk out my words by loving them in very practical ways. I spend hours upon hours of my personal time counseling, listening, loving, and genuinely caring for them. I have been known to be at work very early in the morning, and the maintenance crew has sometimes opened my office door after ten o'clock at night to find me in an inner healing session with one of my kids.

It has been absolutely amazing to watch as these hungry, passionate, radical people come into my office and open up their lives to me. I am completely humbled and yet honored that they would trust me enough to pour out their hearts and souls in an attempt to be known and loved. I have watched over the years as these incredible revivalists have persevered through identity issues, pressed through father and mother wounds, struggled beyond financial restraints, and walked proudly across the stage on graduation night. As long as the Lord allows me to stay in this place, I will continue to serve these amazing students.

I often tell my students that in order to be a great leader, you must first learn how to serve. Jesus said it best when talking to His disciples. In a particular chapter in Matthew, the disciples were arguing about who was the greatest. Jesus, knowing the condition of their hearts said,

> You know that the rulers of the Gentiles lord it over them, and their high officials exercise authority over them. Not so with you. Instead, whoever wants to become great among you must be your servant and whoever wants to be first must be your slave. (Matt. 20:25–27)

What's Love Got to Do With It?

Being a true servant of the kingdom has given me the ability to go beyond my life experiences and to see a much bigger picture. The circumstances of my life could have set me up for complete isolation; certainly, they did not provide fertile soil for a servant's heart to grow and flourish. But the greater truth is that we are all created to serve. Serving a vision bigger than myself gives me the courage to face life with all its twists, turns, mountains, and valleys.

Chapter 17

What's Love Got to Do with It?

On August 8, 2004, I reentered the education world by enrolling myself at the local community college. I had not been in school for over twenty-six years. Immediately, I noticed that I was the oldest person in all of my classes, which made me feel a little self-conscious. I felt out of place on campus because the majority of the students were the same age as my children! I struggled with insecurity issues until I walked into my first psychology class. My professor handed out a poem about love on the first day of class, it read,

How noble true love is! How invincible! How pure! How innocent!

Love simply comes, often undetected even by the one overtaken by it mysterious powers.

True love. The lonely covet its reality. The arrogant flaunt its presence. The ignorant snub its wonder.

It is as illogical as anything can be. It is hopeless to describe it and folly to shun it.

The greatest philosophers have sought to define it. Religion has tried to buy it. Many have tried to elude it.

Love is as hopeless to understand as it is impossible to deny. Yet reason and logic are helpless against love, for it is a most formidable foe of the mundane and the average. True love, you see, dares to go places where reason cannot tread. Love sees realities about which philosophy can only hope to dimly speculate.

True love knows what tradition can only distantly remember.

True love draws the least lovable. It can make anyone a hero.

True love is the sustaining power of the universe itself, yet is so lovely that it abides fully in the hearts of those foolish enough to respond to its rapturous invitation to come. (Author Unknown)

After reading this poem that was just handed to me, I settled down with the thought, *"Ha! I am the only one old enough in the class who knows anything about this subject, L-O-V-E, excluding the professor of course!"* It gave me some self-satisfaction knowing that I had just a little more experience than the rest of my classmates. In reality, I just did not like being the oldest one in class. However, over the course of the semester, I quickly realized that I had very little formal training on the subject of love. I had thought I was somewhat of an expert because I had been married for sixteen years, had birthed and raised two children, and had then experienced divorced. But I discovered I still had much to learn.

I was fascinated by the course's in-depth study of this simple, yet complex, four-letter word. Wars have been fought over this little word, *love*. Lives have been lost over it, books have been written about it, studies have researched it, songs have been sung about it, and complete societies have been ruled by it, yet the quest goes on in search of its true meaning.

Human Needs

The instructor went on to teach that day on Maslow's theory of the hierarchy of human needs. In summary, Abraham Maslow taught that we were all born with five basic needs. My instructor used a pyramid chart to explain these needs to the class. The bottom of the pyramid is the first basic need—physical safety or survival. This includes things like food, shelter, and water. When my daughter was born, she cried every two hours for her need to be met; this need made complete sense to me.

The second layer of the pyramid was the safety need, which includes feeling safe and demands touch and assurance. My daughter and son both required a lot of physical touch and needed to be picked up and held every two hours for the first three months of their lives. Therefore, this second need also touched home for me, and I could relate to this being a basic human need. It was the third basic need that caught my attention the most.

Once the first two basic needs are met, we have a basic need for love. This need actually fascinated

What's Love Got to Do With It?

me because when I gave birth to my two children, I thought they were just demanding little creatures who only knew how to cry, eat, and make presents in their diapers for me. They made their needs abundantly clear by wailing at storm-siren volume until they got the attention they were crying out for. I had no idea that they were actually little human beings capable of feeling love. Now that I have been educated, it is my personal belief that even when babies are in the womb they can feel love.

The next layer of the pyramid is the basic need of self-esteem or the need to feel okay about oneself. The top layer completes the structure with self-actualization, which simply means being willing to grow and change. This, as I was taught, is a life-long process. The entire class was very enlightening to me, but what I gained the most from was the revelation that all of humanity is fascinated with and longing for love.

The Meaning of Love

As I bring this book to a close and write my final thoughts, I am still faced with this very powerful question that I debate with myself as to whether or not I answered. It is my firm conviction that the entire world is in search of the answer to this question: What's love got to do with it?

Not only in the American culture, but in every culture of the world, people are looking for love. In the songs that are sung, to the books that are written, and the movies and plays that are attended, the search for true love is an ongoing quest.

Not only are we humans desperately looking for the meaning of love, but we also desire to experience it. One definition of the word *love* is "an emotion of strong affection and personal attachment." The biblical definition of *love* is "God is love" (1 John 4:8). Other religions may have their own unique definition of love, but the fact remains that the entire human race is in search of love. It is my firm belief that God made us with a deep, burning desire to know and be known. I am no expert on this topic, nor do I claim to have all the answers concerning this subject, but I do have an experience to share, as I have done in this book. A wise person once said, "A man with an argument is always at the mercy of a man with an experience." My experience with love is powerful and life-changing.

First Corinthians 13 is the Bible's famous love chapter, but to get the full picture, we must back up and begin with the end of 1 Corinthians 12. In verse 31, Paul writes, "Now eagerly desire the greater gifts" (1 Cor. 12:31). He then continues, "And yet I will show you the most excellent way" (1 Cor. 12:31). Immediately after that, he shifts into his discussion of love. This indicates that the most excellent way is, indeed, love and that we are to eagerly desire love as the greatest of all gifts!

In chapter 13, Paul writes,

> If I speak in the tongues of men and of angels, but have not love, I am only a resounding gong or a clanging cymbal. If I have the gift of prophecy and can fathom all mysteries and all knowledge, and if I have a faith that can move mountains, but have not love, I am nothing. If I give all I possess to the poor and sur-

render my body to the flames, but have not love, I gain nothing. Love is patient, love is kind. It does not envy, it does not boast, it is not proud. It is not rude, it is not self-seeking, it is not easily angered, it keeps no record of wrongs. Love does not delight in evil but rejoices with the truth. It always protects, always trusts, always hopes, always perseveres. Love never fails. But where there are prophecies, they will cease; where there are tongues, they will be stilled; where there is knowledge, it will pass away. (1 Cor. 13:1–8)

Paul then finishes up his power-packed message with a statement that can be seen on plaques everywhere: "And now these three remain: Faith, Hope, and Love. But the greatest of these is Love" (1 Cor. 13:13). When I reflect on love and read the accounts of Jesus as He walked the earth as a human, I see firsthand how I am able to do the very same thing. I am fully capable and equipped to love unconditionally those whom the Lord has graciously put along my journey.

Without love, people would cease to exist. It is the very life source of our being. God is love, and in Genesis, God created humanity by breathing into Adam's nostrils. It says, "The LORD God formed the man from the dust of the ground and breathed into his nostrils the breath of life, and the man became a living being" (Gen. 2:7). God, who is the very definition of *love,* breathed His love into the first human; that means, at the very conception of humanity, we were formed with love. Our very breath is love! No wonder humankind has been in search of love since the very beginning. It truly is the substance we are made of. Love has been with us all along; our problem is not in finding love, but in *receiving* love.

God So Loved the World

You may have seen the popular verse that shows up on placards even in sporting events, "For God so loved the world that he gave his one and only Son, that whoever believes in him shall not perish but have eternal life" (John 3:16). This simple little verse that is taught in Sunday schools throughout the world is anything but simple and little. It is a powerful reminder that the Creator of the universe and the Originator of all life is deeply, passionately, and strongly in love with each and every one of us. The fact that He even knows us so intimately—that He knows the very number of the hairs on our heads—seems so incredible that our finite minds are unable to fully grasp the magnitude of His love for us. It really is mind-boggling to think that He desires to have a personal relationship with each of us.

The popular song written and performed by Tina Turner "What's Love Got to Do with It?" stirs up emotions that reside deep down in each of our hearts. So many of us have experienced hard life situations, and this song poses a question that causes us to come face-to-face with the reality that we are all in search of true love. The multimillion dollar pornography industry has cashed in on those who look for love in all the wrong places. It really is not love at all, but a sorry counterfeit that is the antithesis of love—lust. Love gives in order to benefit others, but lust takes away from others in order to benefit self.

What's Love Got to Do with It?

I began this book with the question of what to do when our personal experiences seem to contradict the promises and truths of God's Word. Here is my answer: Since God is love and His Word is filled with His promises of love, I will search it out until I discover that my life really is not contrary to love. I have shared with you my own personal quest for love, and I can testify that I have found it. I am madly, passionately, deeply in love with the Creator of all things, and He is indeed in love with me.

Often when I feel the pressures of life beginning to overwhelm me, I simply readjust my focus back on the Lover of my soul. One of my favorite choruses is a reminder in these times, and I find myself repeating its lyrics over and over again:

> Turn your eyes upon Jesus,
> Look full in his wonderful face,
> And the things of earth will grow strangely dim
> In the light of His glory and grace1
> I recently wrote a song that sums up how I feel toward my Lover;
> You are so beautiful to me
> And in Your eyes I can see so clearly
> The Love You have for me
> Drawing me deeper to Intimacy
> I long to feel the warmth of your embrace
> Draw me in to that Secret place
> To look upon the beauty of Your face
> Draw me in

In conclusion, in response to the question that marks the pages of our history books and burns in the hearts and minds of all people—"What's love got to do with it?"—I can confidently answer: *absolutely everything!*

What's Love Got to Do With It?

Endnotes

Chapter 3

1   Bill Johnson, ...

2   Hellen H. Lemmel, "Turn Your Eyes Upon Jesus," (1922); http://www.cyberhymnal.org/htm/t/u/turnyour.htm (accessed March 10, 2012).

Chapter 9

1   Eric Johnson and Bill Johnson, *Momentum: What God Starts Never Ends* (Shippensburg, PA: Destiny Image, 2011).

Chapter 17

1   Hellen H. Lemmel, "Turn Your Eyes Upon Jesus," (1922); http://www.cyberhymnal.org/htm/t/u/turnyour.htm (accessed March 10, 2012).